HARBY
village life in the Vale of Belvoir

Published by the Harby History Group: John Blundy, Cherry Booth, Trevor Coy, Leslie Cram, Neil Cunnington, Anne Dames, Rex Stapleford, Bella Towers and Don Whittaker.
www.harby.co.uk.

Edited by Leslie Cram MA AMA FSA

Designed and printed by
Central Print, Leicestershire County Council.
Typeset in Gill Sans MT 12 point.

FOREWORD

Every community has a history but many are never published in a readable or accessible format. The Harby History Group is therefore to be congratulated in compiling the book Harby: village life in the Vale of Belvoir and producing it in such a short space of time. Synthesising published and documentary sources alongside photographs and oral reminiscences, the book brings to life the story of the village over a thousand years, in a way that will interest both long established inhabitants and more recent arrivals.

Some community history groups come into being through the undoubted enthusiasm of a few individuals but their research and hard work never comes to fruition. There is always a danger that archives and photographs disappear and are not passed on to future generations. This is certainly not the case with the Harby History Group, as not only have they produced this excellent publication, but they have ensured that archives discovered have been deposited in the Record Office for Leicestershire, Leicester and Rutland and photographs scanned for the Record Office, Melton Museum and the village website. In this way the raw materials of history are preserved for future generations to enjoy and use. No doubt the publication of this book will lead to further discoveries and I would urge that they too are preserved and made more widely accessible to others.

The book shows the value of preserving our local heritage: photographic, archival, oral and built before it is disappears. In this way it fosters a vital sense of community within the village. The approach of the Harby History Group in ensuring that unknown documents, photographs and reminiscences are not lost to posterity is to be commended to other communities. Harby: village life in the Vale of Belvoir should be used as an exemplar for others to follow. The work of the Group has already been acknowledged by the award of a grant by the Marc Fitch Fund and wider recognition will no doubt follow with the publication of this volume.

I hope this publication is just a start and will stimulate others to carry out further research, be it into the history of their house, family or other aspects of the local community. In this way Harby: village life in the Vale of Belvoir will have fulfilled its objective of ensuring that the past is preserved for the future.

Mark Dorrington

ISBN 978-0-9567515-0-8

© Harby History Group 2010. All rights reserved. No part of this publication may be reproduced or transmitted in any way or by any means, including electronic storage and retrieval, without prior permission of the Harby History Group and copyright holders.

CONTENTS

FOREWORD   2

CONTENTS   3

INTRODUCTION   5

ACKNOWLEDGEMENTS   6

FACT FILE OF DATES AND HAPPENINGS   7

HARBY THROUGH THE AGES   9

1086 The Domesday Book. 1622 Description by William Burton. 1790 Map by Thomas Gee. 1793 Enclosure award map. 1795 Account by Nichols. 1815 Natural history by George Crabbe. 1846 White's directory. 1850 Thomas Kemp memoires. 1861 Drake's gazetteer. 1871 Census details interpreted. 1884 Map. 1899 Wright's directory. 1904 Map. 1912 Account by Edith Buxton. 1920s Description by Eli Coy. 1928 Kelly's directory. 1930 Map. 1930s William Coy by Henry Coy. 1940s Memories by Betty Holyland. 1941 Kelly's directory. 1944 to 1963 Memories by Wendy Starbuck. 1952 Map. 1944 to 1975 Memories by Tom Sadler. 1971 Map.

ASPECTS OF HARBY LIFE   59

1 HARBY AT WORK   59

BLACKSMITH AND BUILDING. The diaries of Martin Stead edited by Rex Stapleford. Building – Leslie Cram. CANAL. The Grantham canal history and restoration – Hugh Marrows. Tom Watchorn – Idler. CHEESE MAKING. Watson's Dairy – Mary Evelyn. Harby Farmers' Dairy – Trevor Coy. DOCTORS AND NURSES. Health care in Harby – John Blundy. Melton Home Help Service. – The Good Samaritans – Molly Whittaker. The Old Willow Tree – Molly Whittaker. FARMING. Farms at Harby in the 1950s – John Blundy. A Harby farming family – Leslie Cram. Sheep farming in Harby in the 1930s – Harry Kemp. The Gleaners – Betty Holyland. August – Betty Holyland. IRONSTONE MINING. Ironstone and the incline – D L Franks. LACE MAKING. Lace making in Harby – Leslie Cram. Chenille working – Jim Fisher. PARISH COUNCIL The parish council – Anne Dames. POLICING. The village policeman at Harby – John Blundy. THE RAILWAY. Harby and Stathern station – D L Franks. RETAILING. Village shops – Peggy Shipman. Home shopping at Harby 1940s to 1960s – John Blundy. WINDMILLS. Harby windmills – Leslie Cram.

2 HARBY IN THE WARS   105

FIRST WORLD WAR. 1920 War Memorial story – Neil Cunnington. The British Legion – John Blundy and John Dewey. SECOND WORLD WAR. Royal Observer Corps – Rex Stapleford. O-Orange remembered – Dora Butcher. Personal memories of Langar airfield – Rex Stapleford. Jam and Jerusalem – Minutes in time. AFTER THE WAR. Langar airfield and industrial estate – Rex Stapleford.

3 THE SCHOOL   121

The early school – Leslie Cram. The construction and management of Harby school – Neil Cunnington. Mr Edwards – Leslie Cram.

Harby: Village life in the Vale of Belvoir

4 THE CHURCH 128
Graveyard verses. History of Harby church – Rev Norman. Harby parish almanack 1888 – Rev Norman. Come to church letter about 1910 – Rev Stone. St. Mary's Church incumbents – Leslie Cram.

5 THE CHAPEL 136
History of Harby methodist chapel – Nora Blaze.

6 HARBY WOMENS INSTITUTE 139
History of Harby Women's Institute – Minutes in time. Harby WI November meeting – Molly Whittaker.

7 THE READING ROOM /VILLAGE HALL AND VILLAGE MAGAZINES 144
Harby remembered – the Reading Room – anonymous. Later history of the institute – Leslie Cram. Village magazines – Leslie Cram.

8 PUBLIC HOUSES 147
History – Leslie Cram.

9 SCOUTS AND GUIDES 150
History – Leslie Cram. My first camp – Nicola Biggadike.

10 SPORT 153
Harby Cricket Club – Rex Stapleford. Cricket in the rain – newspaper report. Football – Leslie Cram. Harby Football Club – Molly Whittaker. Fox hunting – Gone to Earth – Betty Holyland. Skating – Leslie Cram. Tennis – Leslie Cram.

11 EXCURSIONS 163
Day trips and excursions – Minutes in time.

12 CELEBRATIONS 165
The Horticultural Show – Minutes in time. Harby Feast – Nora Blaze. Harby Feast as it used to be – Edith Buxton. A feast of flowers – Minutes in time. Harby Coronation firework display – Nottingham Guardian.

13 HOME LIFE 170
Joan Watson's diary 1969. Some quiet thoughts – Tom Sadler.

NOTES ON THE CONTRIBUTORS 176

SOURCES FOR THE HISTORY OF HARBY 178

INDEX 180

INTRODUCTION

Harby today is a village in the Vale of Belvoir, in north east Leicestershire, of about 850 men, women and children living in about 380 houses. It has a village school, village hall, a combined garage, teashop, post office and general store, a pub, a parish church, a Christian Fellowship and allotment gardens. The disused Grantham Canal, with a stretch designated a Site of Special Scientific Interest, runs to the north of the village. A network of footpaths extends into the surrounding fields, hedgerows and copses.

What was it like living in Harby in the past? This book tells us. It is an anthology of words and pictures left to us by people from the past. These people range from the agents of William the Conqueror visiting to put together the account in the Domesday Book, to the village blacksmith writing his diary in the 1920s, Harby villagers writing poems, the staff of the Ordnance Survey with their papers and instruments producing village maps, and Harby people taking photos of their weddings, cricket matches and working lives.

The book stops at 1975, a generation ago. It deliberately leaves the opportunity for others to cover Harby in recent years and for a more academic history.

The impetus behind the book was a small group of Harby people wanting to save their family photos for future generations by depositing copies in the Record Office for Leicestershire, Leicester and Rutland. In consultation with the Record Office staff, this was done by making the highest quality digital copies. Albums of original photos can get lost in being passed from generation to generation. Digital copies on discs, like early music recordings on wax cylinders, soon become irretrievable as technology develops. But the Record Office storage ensures the preservation of the image. Over 1,000 images have been passed over and the photos in this book are chosen from those in the Record Office. Recording when and where the photograph was taken and the names of the people has been more time consuming than the digital scanning. Early papers such as diaries were discovered and these have been saved as well. The Harby History Group was John Blundy, Cherry Booth, Trevor Coy, Leslie Cram, Neil Cunnington, Anne Dames, Rex Stapleford, Bella Towers and Don Whittaker. The team also put copies of the photographs onto the village website www.harby.co.uk for people all over the world to enjoy now. Having made copies available in the Record Office for Leicestershire, Leicester and Rutland and on the website, we turned our interest to producing this book. We have reproduced all the images in the text in black and white in keeping with the majority of the early photographs. Many photographs have been digitally edited by Leslie Cram to improve the quality and remove dust and scratches. There are numerous extracts from early descriptions of the village; the idiosyncrasies of the spelling have been kept.

ACKNOWLEDGEMENTS

We are indebted to the people of Harby, some living in the village now, some whose ancestors came from the village, for the loan of the photographs. The original ownership is recorded in the caption under each photograph in the book by the initials of the owner as shown in the following list:-

R E Banks and Freda Fairbrother FBAN, John Blundy JBLU, Dora Butcher DBUT, Cherry Booth CBOO, BCLA, Henry Coy HCOY, Trevor Coy TCOY, Leslie Cram LCRA, Neil Cunnington NCUN, Anne Dames ADAM, Betty Holyland BHOL, Sydney Leleux SLEL, John Mackley JMAC, Vic Millington VMIL, Parochial Church Council PCC, Pat O'Brien POBR, Marion Potter MPOT, Tom Sadler TSAD, Rex Stapleford RSTA, Bella Towers BTOW, Julie Walton JWAL, Joan Watson JWAT, Don Whittaker DWHI, Joyce Wright nee Brown JWRI.

Thanks go to those who worked so hard reading through the text of the book checking the spelling and looking for inaccuracies:- Christine Booth, Claire Brown, Gillian Clark, David Cram, Mark Dorrington, Jonathan and Kate Ford.

We are especially grateful for financial assistance by donations from the Marc Fitch Fund, Long Clawson Dairy, Clawson, Hose and Harby Parish Council, John Deere and RES Tractors. All other costs have been covered by the Group members who gave many hours of their time and the use of their existing computers and photographic equipment.

FACTFILE OF DATES AND HAPPENINGS

850 The village is founded by settlers from Scandinavia about this time.

1086 Domesday Book gives the first written record of the village.

1220 The earliest priest in the parish church is recorded.

1790 The large open fields of Harby were enclosed.

1798 The canal opened.

1827 The first village school was built about this time.

1828 The windmill was built by the Grantham Canal near Colston Bridge.

1839 The Duke and Duchess of St Albans were married in Harby Church.

1846 Forty-nine of the parish had recently emigrated to Australia and other places.

1847 The Methodist chapel was built.

1851 Many young girls are recorded in the census as lace making.

1860 The present Harby School was built.

1876 The church underwent extensive restoration.

1879 The railway opened.

1880 The inclined tramway opened bringing ironstone down to the main line.

1914 – 1918. Nineteen young men of Harby were killed in the First World War.

1920 The War Memorial was erected.

1925 The Men's Institute opened, later called the Village Hall.

1927 The Women's Institute began.

Harby: Village life in the Vale of Belvoir

Factfile of dates and happenings

1936 The canal closed.

1938 Harby windmill went out of use.

1939 - 45. Two young men of Harby were killed in the Second World War.

1942 Langar airfield was built in the Second World War, used at first by the aircraft manufacturer A V Roe and the RAF, then from 1943 by the Ninth American Army Airforce.

1952 The Royal Canadian Airforce came to Langar airfield.

1960 The railway and the inclined tramway closed.

1963 The Canadian Airforce left Langar.

1968 A V Roe left Langar airfield.

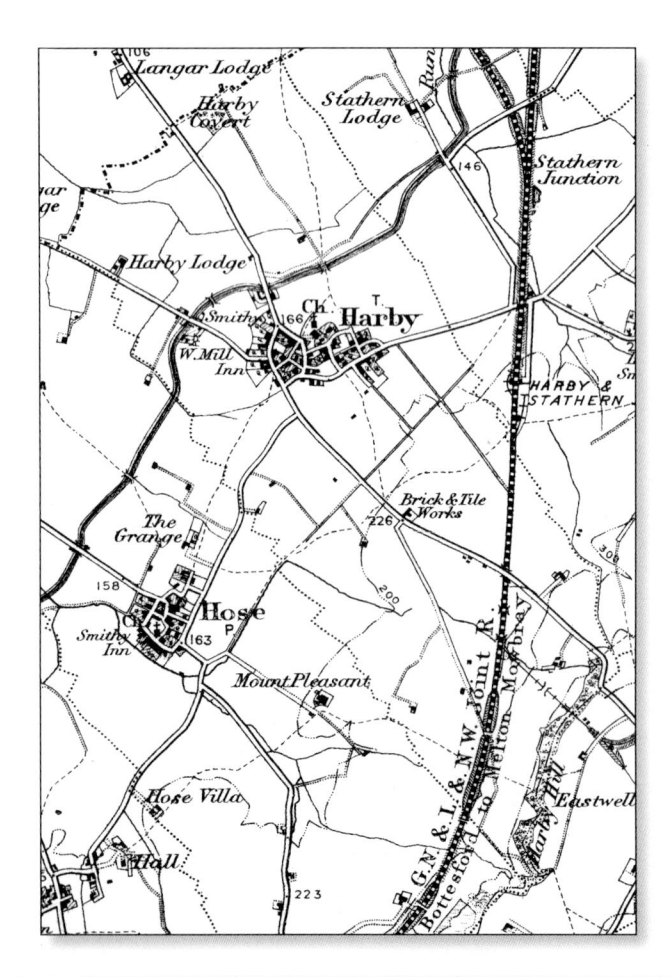

The Ordnance Survey 1 inch to the mile map of 1906 showing the whole of the parish of Harby. The adjoining parishes are Langar on the north, then Stathern east, Eastwell south and Hose west. The parish boundary is shown by a dotted line which merges with the county boundary at the north.

HARBY THROUGH THE AGES

1086 THE DOMESDAY BOOK. *Leslie Cram*

The earliest written reference to the village of Harby is in the Domesday Book which William the Conqueror commissioned to give him a record of who owned which land and what it was worth in his new kingdom. The Domesday Book is written in Latin. The entry for Harby can be translated as:-

"Robert of Tosny owns 17 carucates of land at Harby. In the time of King Edward it was 14 ploughs. Three of these carucates are held directly by Robert with 8 slaves. 13 of the ploughs are leased to 24 freemen, 7 villagers and 3 smallholders. There are meadows measuring five furlongs long and 4 furlongs wide. This land now brings in £5 a year; it used to be worth £4.

"Robert of Bucy owns 1 carucate of land at Harby and leases it to Gerard. The land takes one plough to work it. Gerard sub-leases it to 2 freemen and 3 smallholders. Its value is 5 shillings."

To put all this into English of today - There are 2,160 acres of land which are owned by two French noblemen, Robert of Tosny and Robert of Bucy. Robert of Tosny has 2,040 acres. In King Edward's time, before William the Conqueror took over England, it took 14 plough teams (the plough and eight oxen to pull it) to work this land. Robert has a central farmstead that he runs himself with 8 slaves. The rest of the land is let out to 34 men, 24 of them freemen, 7 villagers, and 3 smallholders. The meadows of the village measure 1000 metres by 800 metres. The rent is now £5, it used to be £4. Robert of Bucy owns 120 acres and lets the land to Gerard. Gerard then sublets it to 2 freemen and 3 small holders. There is one plough team working it. It has a rental value of five shillings.

Putting all these people together it makes up 47 working men. We can assume that each working man had a family of a wife and two children. That would make a total population of Harby in 1086 of about 150 men, women and children. There were 120 oxen. And King William could expect to get £5 and five shillings a year from the village.

1622 A DESCRIPTION OF THE VILLAGE

William Burton from "The Description of Leicester Shire: Containing Matters of Antiquitye, Historye, Armorye, and Genealogy" page 27.

Harby, in olde deedes written Herdeby in the Hundred of Framland, standing in the Vale of Bever upon the border of Nottinghamshire. In the 20. yeere of Edward the third, William Lord Ros, and John de Oreby held lands heere. In the 44. yeere of Edward the third, Roger Delaware was Lord of this Mannor. In the 25. of Henry the eight the Lord Delaware was Lord of this Mannor as it appeareth by an Inquisition taken after the death of Sir John Digby Knight, in the said 25. yeere of Henry the eight, where it was

Harby: Village life in the Vale of Belvoir

found that the said Sir John Digby held 4. messuages (with the appurtenances in Harby) of the said Lord Delaware, as of his Mannor of Harby. In this Towne was borne Jeffrey de Hardby a famous Divine, brought up in Oxford, and after became one of the Canons of the Abbey of Leicester; from whence hee came to be Confessor to King Edward the third, and was by him made one of his Privy Councell of state. He wrote many bookes of speciall note in Divinity, and died in London, and was buried in the Austin Fryers. Here also was borne Robert de Hardby, a Frier Carmelite in Lincolne, who wrote something in praise of the saide Order. The new Patron of this Church is Francis Earle of Rutland. This Rectory is valued in the Kings bookes at 20 pounds.

1790 MAP BY THOMAS GEE

This is the section showing the village of Harby from "A plan of the manor and parish of Harby in the county of Leicester taken in the year 1790 by Thomas Gee". The image is reproduced here by Courtesy of His Grace the Duke of Rutland from the copy held in the Record Office for Leicestershire, Leicester and Rutland, reference PP371. The scale is approximately 26 inches to the mile. The map is orientated with north at the top. The roads, streets and paths of the village are much as today, except that this map shows a road or path going round the edge of the churchyard. The orchards in the village are shown, and the buildings of the three public houses of the Marquis of Granby, Nag's Head and White Hart. The line of the canal with its towpath, which was being surveyed at this time, is shown cutting across the existing layout of the fields with their ridge and furrow strips. Names written across plots of land show the ownership. The plots are numbered but with apparently three separate sequences. The round pinfold is shown on Pinfold Lane. A windmill is shown on the road to Hose on an extension to this section but there are no windmills in the village of Harby.

1793 ENCLOSURE AWARD MAP

This is a section from the enclosure map of 1793. The image is supplied by, and reproduced by kind permission of the Record Office for Leicestershire, Leicester and Rutland, reference number MA/EN/A/136/1. The scale is approximately 16 inches to the mile. The map is orientated with north at the top.
The map is not easy to interpret as it was drawn firstly with the roads, houses and fields from before the enclosures, then proposals for the enclosure alterations were added. Cracks have developed in the surface of the map over the years which can be seen as wavy lines. There is less detail given than in the 1790 map. The road running north to Langar can be seen as straight lines superimposed on earlier lines. There are lines which suggest that the route of the canal is included which was being surveyed at this time. This is the northern of the two maps which cover the parish. This northern map stops at the southern end of the village with only the north side of Stathern Road marked. The roads, streets and paths of the village are much as today, but this map shows a road or path going round the edge of the churchyard, and there are roads extending Boyers Orchard to the east and going north from the turn of Pinfold Lane to buildings at the north-east of the village which are not shown on the 1884 map.

Harby through the ages

Map 1790

Harby: Village life in the Vale of Belvoir

Harby through the ages

Map 1793

12 Harby: Village life in the Vale of Belvoir

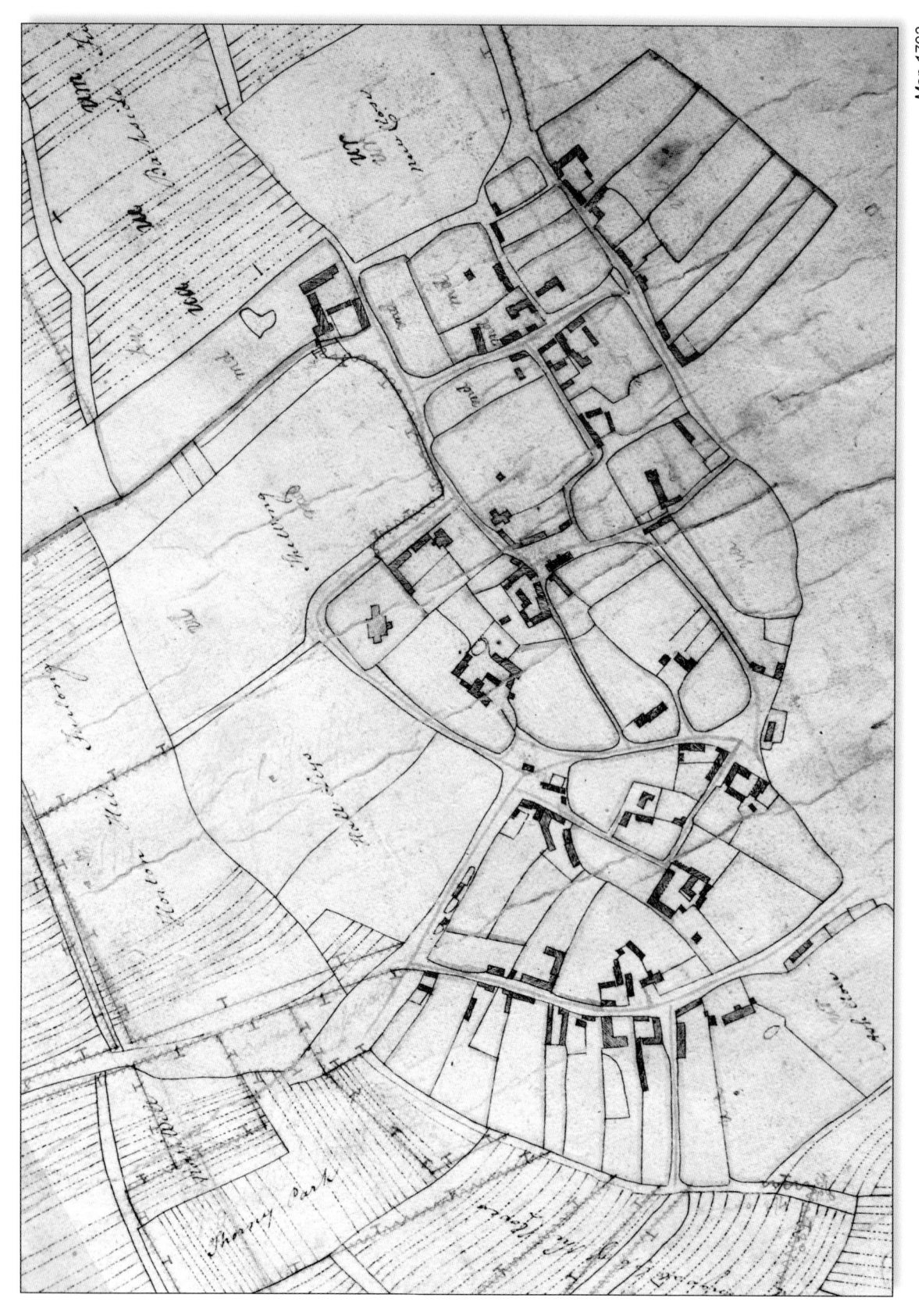

1795 AN ACCOUNT OF HARBY

John Nichols from "The History and Antiquities of the County of Leicestershire" pages 211 – 212.

Harby, like many other villages in the Vale of Belvoir is destitute of woods and streams; no high road leads through or beside it. A heavy clay spreads over every acre in the parish and the uniform operations of husbandry give a sameness to the country, which a stranger might view with disgust; but cultivation has made it fruitful, and its inhabitants feel no envy at the variety of other soils, where the sterility of one part may balance the luxuriance of another. Industry here makes the prospect, and the produce alone is the beauty of the soil. There are about 1800 acres in the parish; and, whilst the field continued open, the method of tillage was, first year fallow; second, barley and wheat; third, beans and pease. The families of Harby are 60, its inhabitants 322, among whom are many small freeholders. There is no mansion or antient building in the village; but the present rector has lately built a neat and convenient house, the probable residence of his successors.

An engraving of 1791 of the cross at Harby with the church and Belvoir Castle in the background. In Victorian times it was moved into the churchyard. After the First World War it was moved again to become the war memorial. From Nichols volume 2, plate XLII, page 212.

Harby church in 1791 seen from the south west. From Nichols volume 2, plate XLII, page 212. The building on the right is the rectory of the time.

Harby Church font about 1800. From Nichols volume 2, figure 10, page 212.

Harby: Village life in the Vale of Belvoir

1815 NATURAL HISTORY *George Crabbe*

George Crabbe, chaplain to the Duke of Rutland, wrote a chapter on "The Natural History of the Vale of Belvoir" in the first volume of John Nichols "History and Antiquities of the County of Leicestershire" pages 191 - 208 and plates 7,8 and 9. This is his description of the mammals and birds.

The Mammalia of the Vale of Belvoir are not perhaps sufficiently distinguished by any form or property to merit a peculiar description. The labouring Horses are large and heavy, and their prevailing colour is black; the Cows are of a middle size, and of the horned breed. The Sheep are less than those of Lincolnshire; yet large, and yearly improving from the breed introduced by Mr. Bakewell of Dishley, a gentleman who is much celebrated for his attention to this part of rural economy.

The Chace-deer belonging to the Duke of Rutland range in considerable numbers over the Vale and the adjacent parts of the Hill country; yet, through the liberality of the family, and their regard to the interests of the farmer, they are fewer than in former times, when the tillage of the soil was loaded with the heavy expence of nightly watchmen for the preservation of their crops.

The remaining animals, which, being Ferae Natura, are yet not considered as common right, are Hares and Rabbits; the former are found plentifully in most parts of the Vale; and the latter, of a very fine kind, at the foot and along the declivity of the hill which leads from the Castle to the parish of Stathern.

This and the neighbouring hill-country are celebrated for hunting, and many Foxes are found here. In the river Devon is sometimes found the Otter, but this happens rarely; and Badgers have been taken, but not often, in the woods of Barston and Stathern.

The Fitchet, or Polecat, makes its usual devastation in this country, and, with the Weasel and Stoat may be frequently met with.

1846 DESCRIPTION OF HARBY
William White from "History, Gazetteer, and Directory of Leicestershire" pages 246 – 7.

HARBY, a considerable village, pleasantly situated in the Vale of Belvoir, on the south side of the Grantham Canal, 8 miles N. of Melton Mowbray, and 12 miles S. E. of Nottingham, has in its parish 629 souls, and 1910 acres of land, of which 880A. is arable, 975A. pasture, 46½A. fox cover and plantations, and 8½A. canal. During the last two years 49 of the parish have emigrated to Australia, &c. The soil is chiefly a heavy clay, and the surface flat. The Duke of Rutland is lord of the manor, anciently called Herdebi, but part of the land belongs to Thos. Manners, Esq., and the Orson, Shipman, Musson, Dunmore, and other families. The manor has been held by various families, and was sold by Andrew Collins, in 1642, to the Earl of Rutland, though part of it was held, in 1086, by Robert de Todenei, the first Norman lord of Belvoir. The CHURCH (St. Mary) is a neat structure, with a square tower, containing four bells and a clock. The latter was given by the Duke and Duchess of St. Albans, in commemoration of their marriage, which was solemnised here May 29th, 1839. They also gave £30, which is invested at interest for the use of the poor. The interior of the church was fitted up with a new pulpit and sittings in 1834, and the stove was the gift of E. B. Hartopp, Esq., in 1841. The rectory, valued in K. B. at £20, and in 1831, at £497, is in the patronage of the Duke of Rutland, and the incumbency of the Rev. Wm. Evans Hartopp, M.A., who has a neat residence, and 455A. of land, awarded, in lieu of tithes, at the enclosure in 1790, when 16A. 2R. 35P., was allotted for the repairs of the church, and is now let for £24. 10s. to five cottagers. The National School was built by the rector a few years ago, and here is a Wesleyan Chapel. On the canal is a wharf, with large granaries, built in 1836. The poor have about £8. 8s. a year from Chester's Charity, and the interest of £10, left by the Rev. John Major, in 1739. The parish feast is on the Sunday after September 19th.

Adcock Mr John
Burnham Wm. schoolmaster
Garton Thomas, police officer
Gibson John, stone mason
Goodson Thomas, clerk
Hallett Geo. vict. Marquis Granby
Hartopp Rev Wm. Evans, M.A., Rectory
Haywood John, vict. White Hart
Julian Richard, maltster
Lamin Henry, baker, &c.
Orson Mrs Ann
Welch John, tailor
Whittle John, vict. Nag's Head
Wright Edward, surveyor of Grantham canal, and coal dealer

Blacksmiths.
Hall Edmund
Kemp Thomas
Kemp Wm.

Boat Owners.
Gregg Samuel
Smart Wm.

Corn Millers.
Bonser Henry
Lamin Thos. (and wharfinger)

Grocers, &c.
Baguley Thomas
Freck John
Dickman Joseph

FARMERS.
* are Owners.
Barlow James
Barnes Wm.
Blount Thomas
*Dunmore Wm.
*Doughty Levi
Freck James
Goodson Robert, Manor House
Hall George
Jackson Mattw. (and butcher)
Kemp Thomas
Musson Mary
*Orson John
*Shipman Wm.
Thompson John
Watchorn Thos.
Watchorn James
Whittle Ann

Joiners.
Hitchcock John, (& wheelwgt.)
Musson Samuel
Musson George

Shoemakers.
Geeson George
Gibson John

CARRIER.
John Hardy, to Melton, Tues. & Nottingm. Sat.

Harby through the ages

MEMOIRES 1850 *Thomas Kemp*

The original handwritten manuscript is held in the Record Office for Leicestershire, Leicester and Rutland, DE 865, generously donated by Barbara Stead, the daughter of the village blacksmith Martin Stead, and is to be seen on the internet at http://www.harby.co.uk/Oldfamily.htm.

The manuscript is written in a bold and fairly legible hand, with various non-standard features making it distinctive. The text is a continuous flow of words not divided into sentences or paragraphs. The original uses no punctuation to indicate sentence-breaks and within sentences capital letters are used unsystematically at the start of words. The spelling is often idiosyncratic and sometimes clearly reflects regional pronunciation.

The transcription is by Leslie Cram. It retains the spelling of the original. Punctuation has been added to break the flow of the text into sentences, with a sentence end indicated by a full stop and a capital letter used to begin the next one. Within sentences capitalisation is used only for proper nouns.

James Kemp was born at Hose in the year 1672. He had two brothers, there father was a farmer. One son was aprentice to a baker, one to a grocer and James to a blacksmith at Harby, with Mr Blanekley. The shop was whe Mrs Musson old houses is in the Nether Street. I can rember the old shop door with brands on it all over, letters as they stampd forck shafts with. James servd seven years there. When he was out of his time he left his old master. He went to Southwell to learn to make geers and chains as horses drawd all in rops at that time. His master was calld Red Hot Tom. He stopd there 12 months. His master died. They sent for him back to Harby, so he began to make geers the first in Leicestershire. In some time he marrie the widow. His eldest son learnt the trade. They made so maney geers they saved a sum of money. They was 4 on them almost night and day.

At that time there was nevee a waggon, never a clock, nor a pump, nor a poor man. The shaft horse had nothing but a cart saddle, no breech. They carts sides come all the lenth and for shafts and at the end of the shafts 4 inche of the end ther was a three quarter hole bored and a pin of wood to fit it. They had a staple put into the hame and a peice of white leather to fit the shaft. So they put this leather ring on the shaft, and then the wood pin throu this. It was cald the towpin. When they took they horse out, they took the pin out, and the ring came of.

This James Kemp eldest son he was called James. He was born in the year 1700. He came a companion with of a yong man, his name was Thomas Gregg. He was born about the same date. These 2 yong men married two sisters the name of Harby of Harby. J Kemps wifes name was Elizabeth. T Greggs wife was Catherine. There father was a farmer and had a house and land of his own at Harby. He gave these two daughters a fortune and the land to his only son John Harby at his mothers death. She was left a widow and her son perswaded to give her house and land to him then and he wold maintain her for

Harby: Village life in the Vale of Belvoir

life. In a few years he died and as there was no written agreement his widow would not pay any think to her so she was destute of house and mantence. James K having a house in the town so these two Good Samaritans put her into this house and maintained her as long as she lived and paid all funerl expnsers betwixt them. This T Gregg hed house of his own in the town. I can git no farthe back of his as I never heard my father say whether he was bor at Harby or a stranger. But I think he was a native of Harby upon having this house of his own. I never heard of him buying it.

Thos Gregg was a sheepherd and lived in his own house. He had 4 sons, Thomas, Richard, John, and Henry, all brought up watching there fleece care.

This J Kemp and T Gregg, there estates joined together and they lived in unitey all the days of there lifes.

Now these two brother was stricken in years, the betwixt seventy and eighty. There was a great election betwix Hungerford and Putchin for the County of Leicester, such a one as never was before nor never since. The Duke of Rutland gave Esqr Putchin his intrust. All them as could not ride on horseback they fetcht in caches and Chaies. There was Plungar, Barkestone, Redmile, and Bottesford, all whent throw Harby. This Mr Gregg and Mr Kemp, as the Duke calld them, for he came acanvisen hisself, so they gave him there votes.

Mrs Gregg and Mrs Kemp told there husbands as they wold never fetch sich old men as them. This is 75 years since.

The day before the election they let them all know to get ready at 8 o'clock on the next morning. Mr Gregg and his wife came to our house about 7 o'clock. In a little wile a man come and to them as the coaches was again Whittles they might come directly. Mr Gregg and my granfather got up, and he said "Now Betty, you said they whould never fetch us". Then Betty and Kate cried. They got into the coch, and ther was sich Huzzas, "Putchin for ever". Old Mrs Hawoodd mother and Mr Julians mother, as they had no votes, pulled off there caps and twirled them over there heads and shouted "Hungerford for ever, Huzza".

There was never seen so many in the Nether Street before, for cochees was seldom seen in those days. Mr Gregg was a verry stout, bulky man, and Mr Kemp was verry stout. There was a man, his name was Richard Hawley, a verey little deformd man, humpd back, but full of concequence. He was put into the coach to Mr Gregg and Mr Kemp. They crushd, he cried, and whould not ride. He whould come out but they snap too the door and away went. My cousin Dickey, for evereybody cald him cousin Dickey, they whould keep him verry warm.

There was open houses at Melton, and on the road the Duke and Lord Granby, Putchin, and all the nobility met them on the road almost 2 mile to welcome them into the town. They was so many carriages and horses that they reached a mile. The gentlemen rode first. There was sich a show as Leicester had never seen. They was well treated, wines, rum, brandy, and anythink as they wishd to drink. Esq. Putchin came to there inn to see if the old gentlemen where good care taken of. Hungerford was voted in. They was brought home to there own door with their hats all over robbins, pleased enough to tell Betty and Kate as they was better look on there than at home.

All thse things was before my day, as my father was 40 years older than me.

The fields was open at that time. It was iclosed in the year 1790. Before the inclosure it being almost all plowd, so we was at work betime in the morning and late at night. We often had 20 pair of plow irons to be done by 6 oclock in the morning so in the middle of the day so my father and my brother James and me sat on an old coffer, so he told us what hapend in his day, and his father told him what whappend in his day, and his fathers. Now my brother could rember nothing. I can rember it as well as if it had been told me yerster day, so my brother James if he wanted to know any think in our family he came to me. I could tell him as well as if I had it in a book before me.

Now this is in my rembrence. I was 3 years and a half old. My granfather and Mr Gregg ushd to sit under a crab tree upon some trees as lay under it, there long stafs in there hands and somtimes. One time Mr Rouse of Hose about there age all sat under this large tree. He was an old compnion of thers, all with there long stafs, about 2 yards long. This puts me in mind of keeping there staf in there hands, as long as live. Tommy was with them. Mr Rouse was telling them as when he was first married he whent to Nottingham with the team, and he brought a peck of tators, the firs as come into Hose. They went again son after and told the man to bring a strike and the Mrs said they should not for they should not eat them, whilst they were good. Mr Rouse lighted his pipe with a glass by the sun.

It was the last time meting. My granfather taken ill and soon died. At is funeral Mrs Gregg stopped at home with my sister Mary and me. She was about half a year old. Mrs Gregg, I rember, knocked her stick on the harthstone to quiet Mary, and said "Churn, butter, churn". Mr Gregg lived but a few months after. Mr gav his son Henry his Estate, to take care of his widow. I have heard my mother say as she was well taken care of, and well used as they was a great to doo with my aunt Kate. She oftimes came to drink tea with us. She was a great favourite of my fathers. My father and mother was at her funerl, and I hope thsee is all gone to happiness. Mr Girton was as good as his promise. His old servant was put into his house and land. There young daughter always lived with them. The eldest son of Mr Gregg and one Mr Leadbetter, both young men, married 2 co heirs at Long Clawson the name of Harby. They an estate at Harby and a good fortune beside. Then this young Mr Gregg took a farm at Sommerby and liv there the remains of his days. The youngest son Henry went to live with Mr Girton of Shelford. He was a faithful servant and livead with him a many years. This Mr had a house and land at Harby. He promised his old servant he should have it when at liberty. This H Gregg married a young woman of Hucknall Torket where the learned Lord Byrons was interd. She was of high blood. She was own aunt to the champin caunt. She was a fine young woman without flattery. Her name was Martha Butler so this coople came to live at Harby with thre father and mother till Mr Girtons house was at liberty.

To the end of there days I was a near neighbour to them and oftimes went in. This daughter was verey kind to her wdowed mother and they lived in peace and comfort. But now her beloved parents is gone to there long home. H Greggs estate blong to his only son Samuel. There was Thomas and Henry but they are gone to the realms above. It is a bewtiful place, it has been new rebilt, it is a paridice. I could speak verry highly of the family but perhaps you whould think I was a flatterer.

And so adieu. Janary 1850. I have seen 74 Christmas Days. T Kemp.

1861 DESCRIPTION OF HARBY
Drake from "Gazetteer and Directory of the Counties of Leicester & Rutland" pages 297 - 8.

HARBY is a large village and parish, pleasantly situated on the south side of the Grantham Canal, in the vale of Belvoir, 8¾ miles N. of Melton Mowbray station, and 14 miles S.E. of Nottingham; containing 640 inhabitants and 1910 acres of land, chiefly a heavy clay. The Duke of Rutland is lord of the manor, but part of the land belongs to Thos. Manners, Esq., and other families. The living is a rectory, valued at £497, in the gift of the Duke of Rutland, and incumbency of the Rev. M. O. Norman, B.A., who has beside a good residence, 455 acres of glebe awarded at the enclosure in 1790, in lieu of tithes. The Church (St. Mary) is a neat building with a square tower, four bells, and a clock, the latter presented by the Duke of St. Albans. Here is a large National School built by subscription, and here is also a Chapel belonging to the Wesleyans. In 1739, the Rev. John Major left £10 for the poor of this parish, who also receive £7. 6s. 8d. per annum from Chester's Charity, (Barkestone.) Mrs. Orson left £20, to which the Duke of St. Albans added £30, the interest of which, with other small charities amounting to about £60, is applied for the benefit of the poor. On the Canal is a wharf, with granaries. The parish feast is held on the Sunday after September 19th.

Post Office at Henry Lamin's Letters from Melton Mowbray, which is also the nearest Money Order Office.

Henry Starbuck aged 8 on horseback, outside Starbuck House in 1867. CBOO.

Harby through the ages

Adcock Mr John
Austin Thomas, tailor
Furmidge Samuel, wharfinger
Gibson John, bricklayer
Haywood John, vict. White Hart
Hitchcock John, joiner and wheelwright
Musson Samuel, joiner
Norman Rev. Manners Octavius, B.A. rector
Watchorn Wm. vict. Marquis of Granby
Wesson George, parish clerk
Whittle John, vict. Nag's Head

BLACKSMITHS.
Hall Edmund
Kemp William

BOAT OWNERS.
Gregg Samuel
Smart William

FARMERS AND GRAZIERS.
Bark Robert
Barlow John, sen.
Barlow John, jun.
Barnes William
Freck James
Goodson Robert, Manor House
Hall George
Jackson Matthew

Kemp Thomas
Karshall John, M. Lodge
Musson Mary
Orson John
Rosling Thomas
Shipman Wm.
Watchorn Thos.
Whittle John

GROCERS, &C.
Baguley Thomas
Dickman Joseph
Dickman William
Freck James
Freck Thomas
Lamin Henry

MILLERS, (CORN).
Bonser Henry
Lamin Thomas

SHOEMAKERS.
Atkins William
Dickman Joseph
Monks James

CARRIERS.
To Melton, Tues; & Nottingham, on Saturday; Samuel Starbuck & Thos. Kemp.

1871 INTERPRETATION OF THE CENSUS OF HARBY *an unidentified author*

The information is taken from the records numbered RG 10/3296 held in the National Archives and was compiled some 25 years ago.

Total Population 539
Children under 16 - 188 (Boys - 86, Girls - 102)
People over 60 - 59 (Men - 26, Women - 33)

Children

There was a total of 188 children under the age of 16 living in the village. They consisted of 86 boys and 102 girls, of these 67 children were under five years of age. There were 23 children under the age of 16 who were out at work. The youngest was a boy of 11 and the next, one of 12, who were agricultural labourers. With the exception of a boy of 15 who was a tailor's apprentice and a boy of 14 who was a horse dealer, all the other boys worked on the land either as farm servants or agricultural labourers. Of the five girls working, one helped her father who was a licensed Hawker and one little girl helped her widowed mother with dressmaking. The rest of the girls were general

Cottage on the corner of Watsons Lane and School Lane in 1876, George Baguley, Stilton cheese maker, in his garden. JWAT

domestic servants. There was a total of 90 children either attending the village school with a certificated schoolmaster, a schoolmistress and an assistant schoolmistress (these being mother and daughter) or being taught by a governess. The latter was a family with 7 children who had their own governess, a girl of 18.

How many of these children stayed at home to study or went to the village school or were sent away to school cannot be worked out.

Working population

Men. From the charts it can be clearly seen that the main occupations of the menfolk of the village are associated with the land, farming and general labouring of the land also associated industries like milling, grazing, corn merchants and the upkeep of canals which were used for the transport of goods and buildings.

There were 16 farmers, 9 farming 100 acres and 9 cottagers. In most cases the sons of the farmers assisted in the running of the farm, and the whole family usually assisted the cottagers. A few of the men had dual occupations such as farmer and innkeeper, clerk and cornmerchant, miller, wharfinger and grazier, grocer, miller and baker.

Women. Unless they were widowed or unmarried, most of the women stayed at home and looked after their families. Opportunities open to girls leaving school were very limited. Jobs were mainly in the domestic line, as general servants to the more prosperous families or assisting parents, either on the land or dressmaking, etc. The schoolmistresses were mother and daughter and the Rector's family as seen from the chart employed 5 women living in to assist the running of the rectory besides the staff who would come in daily.

People over 60. There were 59 senior citizens or old age pensioners, as we would refer to them today. That is, men over 65 and women over 60, of which 26 were men and 33 women. The oldest inhabitant was a man of 84, followed by a lady of 82 and then a man of 81 who was still working as an agricultural labourer. Except for a few cases, the majority of men were still working at 65 and then supporting their families. In the case of women, they usually carried on with the farm or trade, if widowed, or continued in service as a dressmaker, housekeeper etc.

Family names. There were 125 families living in Harby in 1871. Of these there were 21 with 4 or more children. One family had 7 children, 2 sons and 5 daughters, and 3 families had 6 children. There were 11 people living on their own, and 24 families consisting of two people living together. These were usually husband and wife, but sometimes a grandparent and grandchild, or just a parent and child. In a few cases it was found that grandchildren lived with grandparents as, on occasions did nieces and nephews. In a few families there was "living in" help.

The most common family names in 1871 were: COY, FRECK, KEMP, LAMIN, MANCHESTER, MUSSON, SMITH, STARBUCK, WATCHORN and WESSON.

Birth Places. There was a total of 539 people living in Harby in 1871. Of these, 328 were born in Harby, about 60% of the total population. 64 people were born within 5 miles of Harby, 62 within 10 miles, and 30 within 20 miles of Harby. Thus about 90% of the total population were born within 20 miles of Harby. Of the remainder, 16 were born in Leicestershire, 4 in Rutland and 5 in Lincolnshire. Two came from Gloucestershire, 2 from Herefordshire, and one from each of the following: Malvern, Abbots Langley in Hertfordshire, Woolston in Hampshire, Shardlow and Winster in Derbyshire and furthest afield, one from London, Manchester, Elm in Norfolk, Canterbury in Kent and one person was born in Ireland.

It can be clearly seen that the vast majority of people were born locally and never moved very far from their birthplace. Of those who were born further afield, one who was a wife and her mother married to a boatman, two nieces of 6 and one of 13, one a wife of a naval officer, a nurse, a schoolmaster and his wife and child, the children of a foreman, miller and the rector's wife and her mother. It can be seen that these women had met their husbands when they were moving about, because of their work, and likewise, the children were born when the family was moving round.

Size of Village.

The names of the roads in Harby in 1871 were

Burden Lane - 8 houses
Step Lane - 44 houses
Stathern Road - 12 houses
Centre of village - 18 houses
Langar Road - 4 houses

Colston Road - 6 houses
Waltham Road - 4 houses
Hose Road - 2 houses
Rectory - 1 house
Nether Street – 38 houses

Harby through the ages

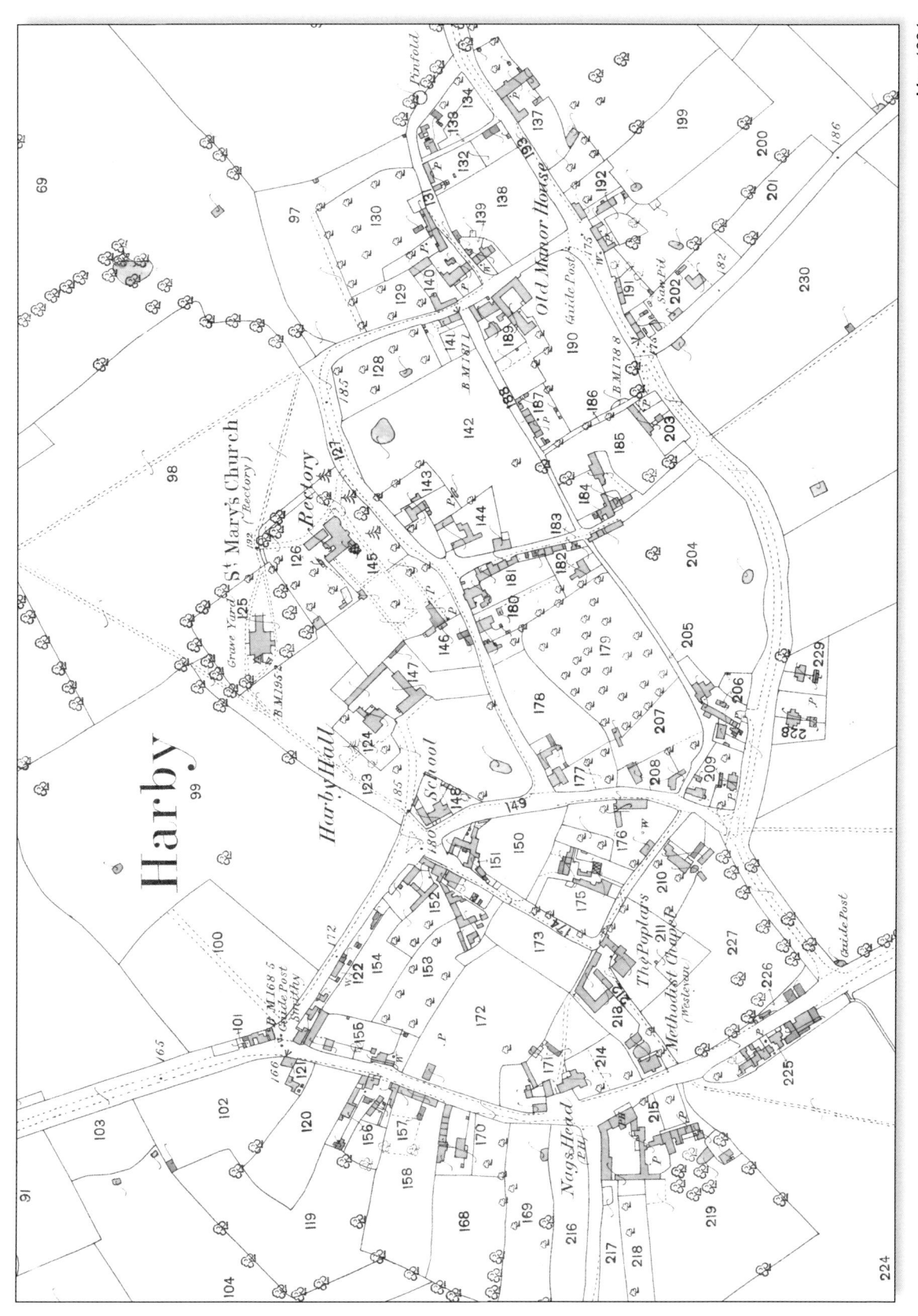

Map 1884

Harby: Village life in the Vale of Belvoir

Harby through the ages

1884 MAP.

This section shows the village from the 1884 1st edition 1:2,500 scale Ordnance Survey map of Leicestershire sheet 7/9. The pinfold is shown in Pinfold Lane, a circular enclosure where any domestic animals found wandering the streets or fields were penned up for the owners to claim. The wells and pumps are shown by W and P; this was before the time of running water in each house. Most of the houses are detached and set in their own gardens. The Smithy is at the corner of School Lane and Nether Street as we call them now, land plot 156. The sawpit is in Green Lane plot 202. The Rectory stands out for the size of the house and its surrounding gardens. By Langar Bridge are the Vale Brewery and a windmill. There is also a windmill at Colston Bridge and on the road to Hose, not shown on this section of the map. There are large areas of orchard in the centre of the village shown by the small trees such as on plots 128 and 129 (our Boyers Orchard) and 204. New opportunities for employment have just begun with the railway opening in 1879 and ironstone mining starting in the hills to the south in 1882. The 1881 census records 11 people working on the railway and one in mining in a population of 591.

1899 DESCRIPTION OF HARBY
C N Wright from "Directory of Leicestershire and Rutland" page 80.

HARBY is a considerable village and parish in the division, union, and County Court district of Melton, and rural deanery and hundred of Framland. The village is on the western part of the Vale of Belvoir, on the south side of the Grantham canal, and border of Notts, 8¾ miles N. from Melton, 14 S.E. from Nottingham, and 24 from Leicester. St. Mary's Church is a fine structure, dating from the Early Decorated period. In 1874-6 the building was well restored, except the tower, at a cost of £1,500 (the chancel at a cost of £500, defrayed by the Rector). The living is a rectory of the nominal value of £569 a year (gross), arising from 459a. of glebe awarded in lieu of tithes at the Enclosure in 1793, with residence, in the gift of the Duke of Rutland. The registers date from 1700. There are Wesleyan Chapel, built in 1847, and National School, erected in 1860. The parish has a fifth portion of the Charity of William Chester, who in 1703 left 68a. of

Stathern Lane about 1900, looking west towards the junction with School Lane. HCOY

Looking north along Nether Street before the First World War. HCOY.

Skaters on the canal near Langar Bridge in 1894. The photograph was taken by James Norman, the son of the rector. POBR

Harby through the ages

land, also the interest of £40, left by the Duke of St. Albans, and of £10 and £20 left by Mr. Major and Mr. Orson. The principal landowners are the Rector, the Duke of Rutland, lord of the manor, and Messrs. F. Orson, J. Smith, J. Whittle and H. T. Shipman. The area of the parish is 1,980a. 3r. 10p.; rateable value, £3,628 1s. (land, £2,093 13s.; buildings, £1,534 8s.); population in 1891, 636. The feast is on the Sunday after September 19th. A station on the joint line of the G.N. and L. and N.W. Companies from Northampton and Nottingham, about a mile distant, serves for both Harby and Stathern.

Parish Council.— Messrs. Wm. Spencer (chairman), J. Whittle, jun., W. Furmidge, G. Kemp, F. Orson, J. Rose, and Wm. Starbuck ; Clerk, Mr. Jas. Stokes.

St. Mary's Church.— Services, Sunday 10.30 and 6.15. H.C. first Sunday in month. Rector, Rev. M. O. Norman, B.A. ; Curate, Rev. A. H. S. Johnson ; Wardens, Messrs. T. Freck and J. Stokes ; Organist, Mr. Thos. Freck ; Sexton, Thomas Hall. Kemble's Hymns.

Wesleyan Chapel.— Services, Sunday 2.30 and 6. Steward, Mr. O. Stokes.

Post, Money Order and Telegraph Office, and Savings Bank.— Mrs. Ann Kemp, sub-postmistress. Letters from Melton delivered at 8.15. Box cleared at 4.55 on week-days. Telegrams 8 to 10 Sundays.

Looking down Watsons Lane from beside the school around 1900. JWAL.

A pony and Mr Thomas Herrick in front of the wall of the Rectory in Boyers Orchard about 1890. NCUN.

26   Harby: Village life in the Vale of Belvoir

Brown James, boot maker ; h. Hose
Buxton Robert, blacksmith
Cox Walter, v. Nag's Head
Dewey John Chas. brewery traveller
Edwards Alfred Warman, master National school
Furmidge & Kemp, brewers ; & at Stathern
Furmidge Mr. Russ
Green William, cheese manufactr
Gregg Misses Elizabeth & Catherine
Hall Thomas, blacksmith & sexton
Haskard Charles, boot maker
Hourd Albert, wheelwright
Johnson Rev. Alfd. Hy. Sml. curate
Kemp George (Furmidge & Kemp)
Lamin Mr. John Lamin & Shipman, millers, corn, coke & coal merchants & wharfingers
Mabbatt George, news agent
Martin Wm. Harvey, baker & flour dlr
Musson Daniel, joiner & wheelwright
Norman Rev. Manners Octavius B.A. Rectory
Robinson Frederick, coal merchant
Sainty Frederick Barron, inland revenue officer
Shipman Wm.(Lamin & Sh.) ; h.Hose
Starbuck James, chimney sweeper
Stokes Otho, plumber & tinner
Swingler Samuel, butcher
Veen Vander Y'bele Gerard, Stilton cheese manufacturer
Welch Alfred, tailor

Whitewoods at the junction of Stathern Lane and School Lane. From a postcard sent about 1910.
NCUN

A postcard dated 1906, looking east along School Lane from Nether Street. The blacksmith's forge is on the right. On the side of the cart is written H Allen Butcher. The road sign points to Waltham and Melton.
NCUN

Harby through the ages

Cottagers & Cowkeepers.
Allen William
Furmidge Samuel
Grigg Thomas
Herrick Thomas
Hopkin James
Kemp Eustace
Martin Thomas, & wheelwright, & implement manufacturer
Musson John, & joiner
Parker William Henry
Rawlinson Charles
Skinner Frederick, & carrier

Dress Makers.
Musson Misses Sarah & Rebecca
Watchorn Mrs. Lavinia
Welsh Miss Mary
Wesson Miss Jn

Farmers & Graziers.
Barke Robert
Freck James, jun Freck Thomas
Cox Walter, & v. Nag's Head
Furmidge Wm. & Kemp George, & coal & corn mchts. ; & at Stathern
Orson Francis
Shipman Henry
Starbuck William, & cab propr. & carr
Swingler William, Harby lodge

Graziers.
Baguley William
Cox Walter, & v. Nag's Head
Jackson John & James, & butchers
James John
Lamin William, Harby lodge
Miller John
Pick Josiah, & cowkeeper
Porter George, & v. White Hart
Rose Joseph
Spencer William
Stokes James, & rate collector
Wright Edward

Grocers & Shopkeepers.
Brown John
Dickman Wm. & coal merchant, trap proprietor, tinner & plumber
Kemp Mrs. Ann, & cottager, & sub-postmistress
Pepper Frederick, & draper
Stokes Miss Jane, & draper & gnl. dlr
Watchorne Henry, & baker

Carriers.
Skinner Fredk. & cottager, to Melton Tu. ; Nottingham S
Starbuck Wm. & farmer, to Melton Tu. ; Nottingham W. & S

Whitewoods where School Lane meets Stathern Lane about 1900, named after the white railings on the right. Girls and boys use these to practise their gymnastic skills. JBLU.

28   Harby: Village life in the Vale of Belvoir

1904 MAP.

Here is the village as shown on the 1904 2nd edition 1:2,500 scale of the Ordnance Survey map of Leicestershire sheet 7/9. The position of the water supply through wells and pumps is shown by W and P on the map. The windmill shown on the 1884 map by Langar Bridge has gone, so has the pinfold in Pinfold Lane and the Vale Brewery is disused. New terraced houses have been put up in plot 157, Exchange Row on Nether Street. Thraves Terrace off Main Street in plot 215 and Rutland Terrace in Green Lane are also new. These new cheap houses are connected with the 28 railway workers and 28 ironstone miners recorded in the 1901 census in a population of 652. The Post Office is marked PO in Watsons Lane. There are allotments on the north and east of the village.

HARBY IN 1912
Edith Buxton from the Harby Beacon magazine, September 1952.

We often sit and think of the days that were. The 'good old days' some people say. No doubt they were good but we have improved in many ways. In the old days the lodge children who came to school had to bring sandwiches and cold tea. Now there are excellent dinners provided - meat, two veg. and a sweet for all who care to pay 7d. At playtime too, each child has a bottle of milk and a straw with which to drink it. There were slates and slate pencils and very few books. We learned to count on a ball frame. Now there are papers, exercise books and dozens of text books and a wireless set.

In the winter evenings we sometimes had a magic lantern show. Magic indeed. I remember Uncle Tom's Cabin being shown and at the end when the lamps were turned up we were all black with smuts and smoke from the smoking paraffin lamps. Today we have the pictures and television. We went to Nottingham once or twice a year and had to walk to the station a mile away. We went to Skegness for the Choir Outing by train. We had 1/- to spend and were passing rich. We bought a pipe for Father (clay, of course) and a box with shells on for Mother, ¼ lb. of sweets for 1d (!) - a donkey ride for 1d and glasses of lemonade at ½d (!!) a glass as well as ½d ice cream cornets. Today the buses take us every week somewhere.

Harby school teachers in 1912, from left to right Miss Buxton who taught the infants, Mr Edwards the Headteacher, Mrs Musson who taught "Inter." POBR.

Harby through the ages

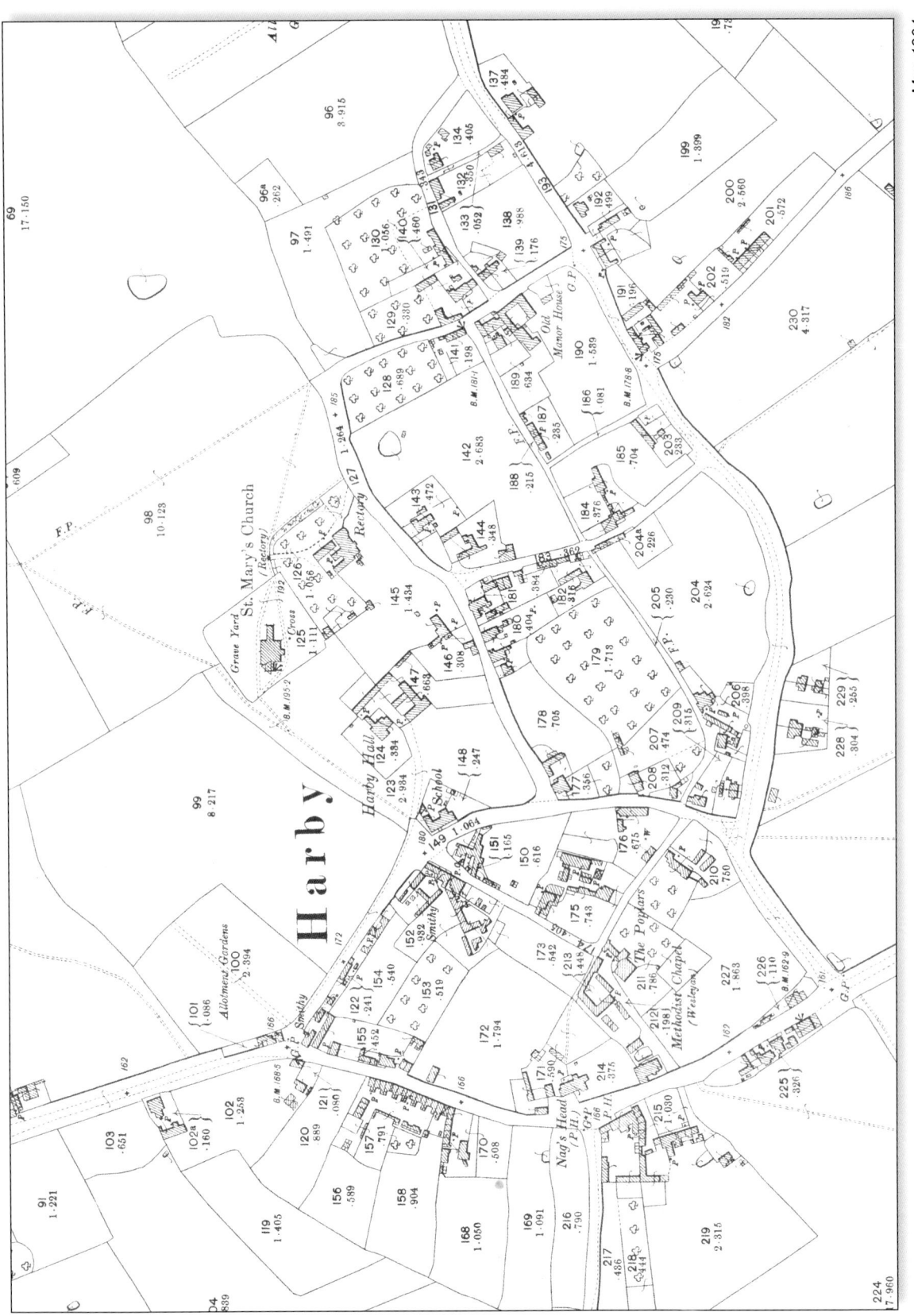

Map 1904

The hounds used to meet in Mr Furmidge's field and Royalty and Nobility gathered there. The 'take off' would be to Harby Covert which is now an aerodrome. There were many horses and carts, bicycles but few motor cars. Today we are all mechanised. We used to glean a good bit of grain for our fowls in the winter. But the modern instruments clean all up. Early to bed was general as lighting was somewhat dim with oil lamps and candles. On very dark nights we went to church and choir practice with a candle-lantern. Now we have our torches and soon we shall have street lighting.

All social events were held in the School as there was no Institute then. Miss Starbuck's Harby Feast Tuesday Concert was the great event of the year together with Mr Pepper's Yeomanry Ball. The policemen were nice and friendly. A few people were taken to court. One policeman I remember had 4 boys who could swear like troopers.

The canal was often frozen over for weeks at a time. What fun we had sliding and skating in the moonlight. Romance began - but the ice thawed before it had time to mature.

People were kind and helpful then with less amenities. But kindness and helpfulness is still to the fore today. Indeed I think nothing will ever obliterate village kindliness - it is proverbial.

On the frozen canal about 1925, possibly near Langar Bridge. FBAN.

HARBY IN THE 1920s
Eli Coy, edited from a tape recording made in the 1970s and published in the Harby News, issue 1, page 12.

To look at, Harby hasn't changed all that much during the 50 or so years since the First World War. At any-rate, the Church and the Chapel were there then as they are today, and so was the School which was run by Alfred Edwards. Mrs. Kemp kept the Post Office in those days, and telegrams were sent off in Morse code. The village had two bakers, two butchers, four shops, the Cheese Dairy and at least three other small cheese-makers. There was a mill too, owned by Mr. Stubbs of Hose, and run by the miller, Wm. Hall.

Harby was well-off for coal too, with three coal merchants, and it boasted the same number of joiners, all by the name of Musson, curiously enough. Mr. Martin was the name of the wheelwright, and his grandson still lives in the same place, and keeps the wheelwright's shop going. Mr. Stead followed Thos. Hall at the blacksmith's shop, and was there for most of the 50 years.

The Nag's Head and the White Hart were important land-marks in the village, as they still are today. They were only open six days a week, but I am told that sometimes the men would call at the pub on the way to work, and be there for the rest of the day, because in those good old days they kept open all day long.

Although we were well-catered for by tradesmen, other conditions were very different from those we know today. There was no electric light, and no piped water, which all came from various pumps and wells in the village, and had to be carried home. In dry weather the supply dried-up and people would have to fetch water from the canal in 17-gallon churns on wheels. There were no proper baths in those days, and when people needed one, they brought a tin bath indoors, and filled it with water from the copper which they used for boiling the clothes. There were no lavatories either, only earth closets placed as far away from the house as possible. To pay a visit in the night meant a long walk to the bottom of the garden; some things have improved at any rate!

Very few of the roads were tarmac'd, and as most were mud-bound, it was a great problem to stop the mud getting into the houses. Nearly every Saturday, the women would swill the causeway in front of their doors, and wore pattens for the job. These were worn on the feet, and had wooden soles with an iron ring under the feet which lifted the wearer and her skirts a few inches above the mud. I was told a story once of grandparents who walked to Nottingham on pattens, and carried home panchions on their heads, but I don't know if it was true.

The Rawlinson's farmhouse at the corner of School Lane and Watsons Lane about 1923. An oil painting by Guilford Wood who was an amateur artist who lived in Lilac Cottage in School Lane in the early 1920s. It is a fine example of a painting in the naïve style. JWAT.

Horse and cart with two men in 1926. This may be the Furmidges of Hall Farm in a field sloping down to the canal. LCRA.

Modern transport, of course, was non-existent; it was a case of walking, or of going by pony and trap, or on horse-back. There were a few bicycles, however, but the railway station was one-and-a-half miles from the village. One of the regular walkers to the station was George Moult, the newsagent. Not only did he walk many miles every morning, but he repeated the performance at half-past five with the evening papers. National papers were a rarity in the village, but we had Titbits, Comic Cuts, John Bull, and The News of the World, and at weekends The Christian Herald arrived. On Saturday mornings the Grantham Journal was delivered in the village by Mrs. Jane Brown, who was a real character, and I can see her now with her long dress trailing in the mud and her Welsh bonnet perched on top of her head.

People worked very hard in those days, mostly on the farms, the railways, or the ironstone quarry. A waggoner, for example, would get up at five o'clock in the morning, and his first job would be to feed the horses. After that, he would come home for his breakfast if he lived nearby, or otherwise take it with him; then he would go out to the fields ploughing, sometimes with two horses, sometimes with three, depending on the nature of the land. This would go on from seven o'clock in the morning until perhaps two o'clock in the afternoon. Having had a meal, he would go back to the fields to cut chaff, which was done mostly by hand, and was very hard work. At the end of the day he would have the horses to feed again, and would return later still to bed them down. The next day up at five o'clock again! There was a waggoner on most farms.

The cowman had much the same sort of working day, although he might get up an hour or so later to feed and milk the cows by hand.

Of course, it wasn't all work in Harby fifty years ago. Not for the children, at any rate; they managed to find some fun, especially in winter. I don't know whether I'm imagining it, but the winters then seemed to be far more severe than they do now. The canal seemed to be frozen over from November until March.

Harby through the ages

There was one occasion when the whole village, including a lot of quite elderly people, turned out to slide and skate on the canal. It was full all day long, and at night too when everyone would have lanterns. Anyway, as I say, on this occasion Mr Edwards, the schoolmaster was there. "Now you boys", he said - and there was one piece of ice which was thin where the weeds had grown - "Now you boys, keep away from this hole whatever you do, or you'll be in the water". No sooner had he given the warning, than there was a loud crack, and the ice swallowed him up. Of course the boys and girls thought it was great fun, but it must have been horribly cold for the old boy.

In summertime, too, the canal had its uses in providing amusement for the village. There were fishing matches, and of course the boats. These were real barges, horse-drawn, with refuse from the towns, which was put on the land for manure. The children were always there on these occasions, because if you looked hard enough, you could be sure to find a penny or a sixpence or two, which in those days put them in the millionaire class. They didn't mind the filth a bit.

The swing-bridge was a popular spot in summer for swimming - at least for the male sex. The females kept out of the way, because in those days swimming costumes weren't heard of in the village! The men and boys usually wore a good big handkerchief, folded in half, and tied with string. It served, but some didn't even have that to wear, so on a hot summer's day the female population gave the swing-bridge a wide berth.

The rectory around 1920. An oil painting by Guilford Wood. MPOT.

We had a good cricket team in those days, and matches were played against most of the villages roundabout. You got there by bike or on horseback and on a fine evening there would often be fifty or sixty spectators enjoying the game. Sometimes there was tennis for youngsters on the Rectory Lawn.

People had to make their own recreations, and maybe they enjoyed them all the more for that.

Another winter event in Harby was the Hunt Meet. The huntsmen drove up in their Rolls Royces and Daimlers which are the vintage cars of today - this was almost the only occasion when you saw a car in the village.

The horses and their grooms would come to the Abbey station, a train-load of them. Most people who rode had probably 4 or 5, and even sometimes 6, horses, and nearly as many grooms. The men wore the traditional red coats and white buckskin breeches. When travelling they also wore an apron to stop the whitening rubbing off. The ladies wore their riding habits with a long skirt, silk hat, and a veil. They all rode side-saddle in those days. The grooms (they were called the second horsemen) usually wore livery, some in green, some in black, some in dark blue, all with bright buttons and tall silk hats with a cockade. The cockades were different for each owner, as a rule.

And away they would go, maybe three or four-hundred horses when they went off. It was a wonderful sight, no doubt about that!

1928 DESCRIPTION OF HARBY
Kelly from "Directory of the Counties of Leicestershire and Rutland" pages 97-98.

HARBY is a large village and parish on the borders of Nottinghamshire, on the south side of the Grantham canal, with a station called "Harby and Stathern," which is the junction of the Grantham and Melton Mowbray and Melton and Nottingham joint lines of the London and North Eastern and London, Midland and Scottish railways, 1¼ miles south-east of the village, 8¾ north from Melton Mowbray and 14 south-east from Nottingham, in the Melton division of the county, hundred of Framland, petty sessional division of Belvoir, union and county court district of Melton Mowbray, rural deanery of Framland (first portion), archdeaconry and diocese of Leicester. The church of St. Mary is a building of stone in the Perpendicular style, consisting of chancel, clerestoried nave of three bays, aisles, south porch and an embattled western tower with pinnacles, containing a clock, presented by the Duke of St. Albans, and 5 bells, two dated 1610, one 1614, one 1701 and the fifth 1887: the chancel retains an aumbry and a piscina, and there is also a piscina in the south aisle: the font bears the date 1606: the church was restored and new roofed in 1870, and further restoration took place during 1874 and 1876: a new vestry and organ chamber were added in 1903: there are 220 sittings. The register dates from the year 1700. The living is a rectory, net yearly value £700, including 1 acre of glebe, with residence, in the gift of the Duke of Rutland, and held since 1925 by the Rev. Arthur Evelyn Furnival M.A. of Exeter College, Oxford. In

Harby through the ages

Pinfold Lane about 1930, outside the Walnuts. Mrs Lil Watchorn selling milk from her cows to Mrs Wright & Mr Moulds The Watchorns kept cattle near the railway station and went in the cart with the pony to bring back the milk. BTOW.

Looking from the school down School Lane to the junction with Burden Lane about 1935. NCUN.

Burden Lane about 1935, the Post Office is on the right in the distance. NCUN.

Harby: Village life in the Vale of Belvoir

the churchyard there was an ancient stone cross, now removed to the village green and reconstructed as a memorial to the men of Harby who fell in the Great War, 1914-18. There is a Wesleyan Methodist chapel, built in 1847. In 1739 the Rev. John Major left £10, the interest for the poor of this parish, who also receive £6 13s. 4d. yearly from Chester's Charity, of Barkstone; Mrs. Hannah Thompson left £10 for the benefit of the church Sunday school in 1866; Mrs. Orson left £20; the Duke of St Albans gave £40 in 1839: the interest of the above sums, which are all in the care of the Charity Commissioners, is distributed yearly by the rector and Parish Council trustees. The land is chiefly owned by farmers. The soil is clay; subsoil, clay. The chief crops are beans and wheat and some land in pasture. The area is 2,056 acres of land and 6 of water; the population in 1921 was 619.

Sexton, John Cumberland. Post M. O., T. & T. E. D. Office (within limited distance). Letters through Melton Mowbray
Railway Station (L. & N. E. & L. M. & S) Carriers.- Miller, to Melton Mowbray, tues. & W. Coy runs an omnibus service to Melton, tues.; Nottingham, wed. & sat

PRIVATE RESIDENTS.

Attewell Thomas
Furnival Rev. Arthur Evelyn M.A.(rector), Rectory
Green Mrs
Watchorn John James
Watson Herbt
Whittle Joseph

COMMERCIAL

Marked thus ° farm 150 acres or over.

°Barke Geo. farmer
Bowler Alfred, grocer
Buxton Robert, grazier
Clarke Richard, greengrocer
Coy Danl. plumber
Coy William, carrier, motor omnibus proprietor, motor haulier & coal merchant
Dewey Jas. Akerman, butcher
Dickman Thomas, builder, painter, hot water engineer & plumber
Edwards Alfd. Warman, clerk to Parish Council
°Fairbrother Herbert, farmer
°Furmidge Harry, farmer
Gale Christopher, grassier
Gibbs Fredk. R, farmer
Gray Jsph Wm. market gardener
Harby Farmers' Dairy Ld. (The), cheese mkrs
Havill Walt. Jas. baker
Haywood John, grazier
Hopkins James, grazier
Jones Fredk. White Hart P.H
Jones George F. traveller
Kemp Geo. Clarence, grazier
Kemp Thomas, grazier
Lamin Frank, farmer Lamin John, grazier
Mackley William T. cycle agent
Martin Ernest, wheelwright
Parker William Henry, grazier
Pepper Fredk. grocer, Post office TN 1
Pick Josiah, cowkeeper
°Rawlinson Charles, farmer
Rawlinson Ernest, farmer
Starbuck Saml. butcher TN13
Stead Mabel (Mrs.), shopkpr
Stead Martin, blacksmith
Stokes Otho & Son, plumbers & glazrs
Stubbs Walter, miller (oil engine & wind), The Mill
Sumner James, grazier
Swingler Jesse, farmer, Harby lodge
Tustin Frank Wm. Nag's Head P.H. TN 9
United Dairies (Wholesale Ltd.) cheese makers
Watchorn William, grazier
White Joseph, farmer
Wilford James Corner, farmer

Harby through the ages

Thraves Terrace off Main Street. May Towers at her backdoor about 1930. BTOW.

Starbuck House in Main Street about 1925 with Betty Starbuck on left and Mary Jane Starbuck. CBOO.

1930 MAP.

Here is the village shown on the 1930 4th edition 1:2,500 scale Ordnance Survey map of Leicestershire sheet 7/9. There has been little building of new houses since the 1904 map. The Post Office is now in Burden Lane. The Institute or Village Hall has been erected to the north of School Lane. There are more allotments in land plot 120. Employment continues as before on the railway, ironstone mining, cheese production and farming. Unemployment was a concern in the 1930s but the WI minutes record in 1933 that most of the men have allotments suggesting that there was enough food for everyone. The position of pumps and wells shown on the 1904 map are not shown here although they continued to be the only source of water. Mains water, sewage removal and electricity came in the years after the date of this map.

Harby through the ages

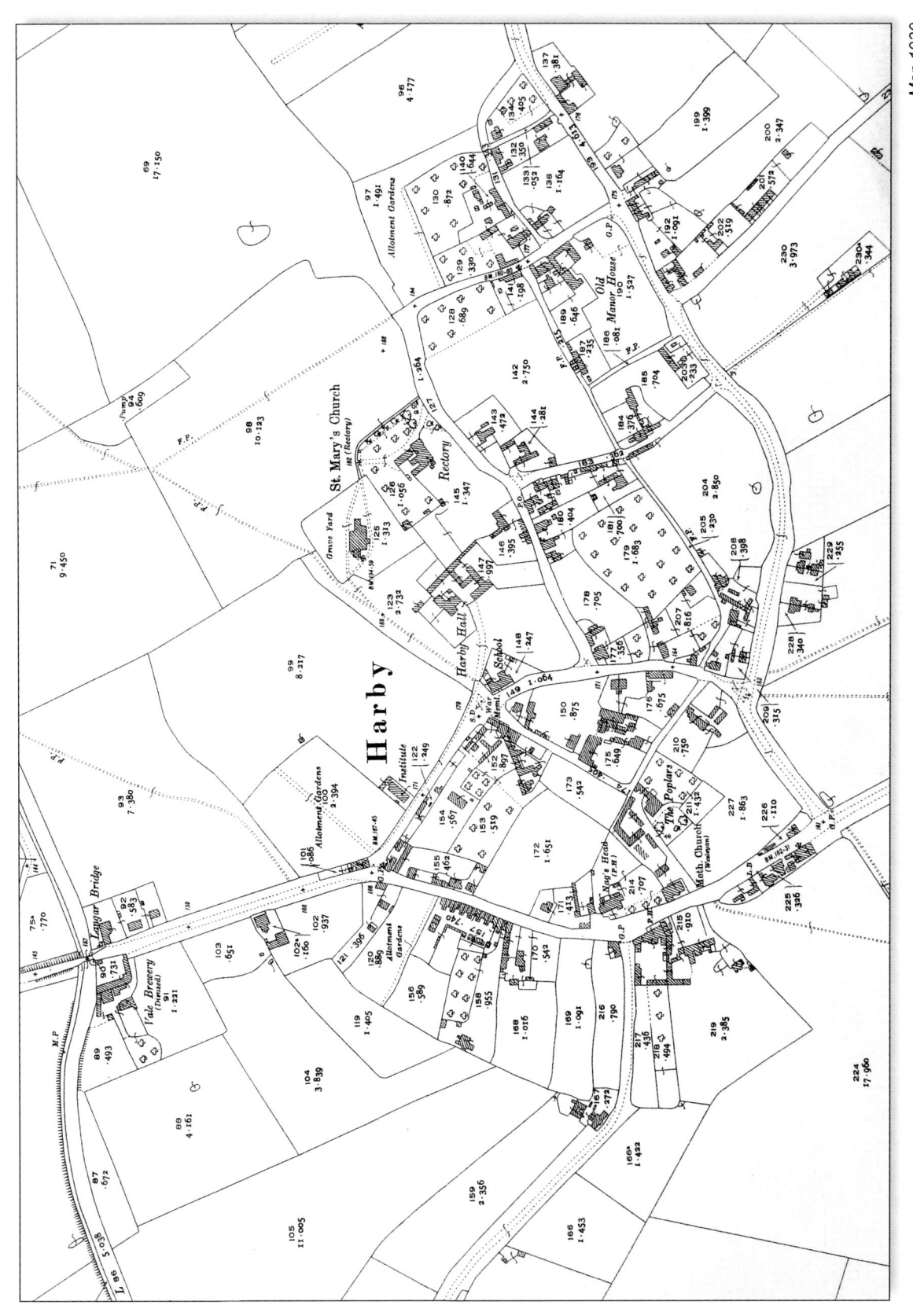

Map 1930

Harby: Village life in the Vale of Belvoir

BUSMAN BILLY - ISAAC WILLIAM COY 1897-1968 *Henry Coy*

William was born at Harby in 1897 to Harry and Elizabeth. In the 1911 census the family, Harry, Elizabeth, Isaac, Mary and Eli lived in Nether Street, Harby, at Diamond Cottage. Harry is shown as a quarryman and William as a Baker's apprentice aged 14. William served in World War 1 with the Northumberland Fusiliers.

About 1921 William, based at Diamond Cottage, started his own business selling coal from a horse and cart. It is likely that his mother had sold coal from the same address previously and William started making deliveries to surrounding villages. The coal may have come from the Nottinghamshire pits by canal barge. Later William extended his business by delivering and collecting goods to and from Nottingham by horse and cart through Colston Bassett and Cotgrave. One of his customers was Colston Bassett Hall. Villagers occasionally asked for a ride on the dray.

The horse and cart was replaced with the famous model 'T' Ford equipped with canvas top and seats to carry passengers when not required for carrying goods. This developed into a local daily bus service from Stathern to the Black Boy Hotel yard in Nottingham. Mr Stead mentions using this service in his diaries. Trips were made to Skegness and local events. The bus service and 4 buses were sold to Bartons Transport in 1935. The retail coal business continued deliveries to local villages until it was sold in 1980.

In 1951 William and son Henry started a Concrete Block Manufacturing Business in the garage at the south end of School Lane where they now lived, known as W Coy & Son (Coycrete) Ltd, and later at the site on Stathern Lane. The blocks were sold to farmers and builders over a wide area. The business was sold in 1975.

Henry Stokes Coy and Mrs Elizabeth Coy outside Diamond Cottage in Nether Street about 1933. HCOY.

Milk was collected daily in churns from local farmers and delivered to Wilts. United Dairies in Harby. Whey was transported in a tanker to Ashbourne. The transport business expanded in the 1960s and transported John Deere Machinery from Langar to their dealers all over the country and to agricultural displays. Machinery was collected from the docks at Liverpool, Hull and Ipswich and brought into Langar or taken direct to dealers.

In public service Isaac was a special constable and later special sergeant which involved duties at local events, assisting the local policeman and also some night patrols around the Vale of Belvoir. No information is available about his length of service but many specials were recruited during the time of the General Strike in 1926.

William was in charge of the local observer corps post J2 on the Hose junction during the Munich crisis and during World War II up until 1945. His duties consisted of preparation of the 24 hours duty rota for the local members of the corps. This would have been a major task as local farmers, businessmen and workers had to be fitted in with their normal work schedules. He would also be required to do a spell of duty watching for friendly and enemy aircraft.

Isaac William Coy aged 18 in a photographer's studio in France about 1915. HCOY.

MEMORIES OF HARBY AROUND 1940 *Betty Holyland*

My grandfather was John Musson, master joiner, wheelwright and undertaker. One of my mother's earliest memories was seeing her father John Musson preparing for the funeral of the Rev. Octavius Manners Norman - a big event with all the grand funeral trimmings as he was related to the Rutlands on the female side of his family. My father was Arthur Butcher Cooper, the cousin of Harry, Horace and Jack, 'Woody' and May Butcher, whose parents were the landlords of the Nag's Head in Main Street in Harby.

The Church was the 'hub' of the wheel around which all the village life revolved. One of the most beloved Rectors that Harby was privileged to have was 'Parson Stone'. He was involved with every man, woman and child. Not a child was born that he did not visit within a couple of days. Two evenings were set aside each week at the Rectory for the getting together of young people, boys one evening, and girls the other, for the purpose of encouraging interests they may not have otherwise have had the chance to pursue. Each Christmas a present for each man, woman and child was provided by him on the village Christmas tree. He had already by this time taken the trouble to find out just what each individual really needed. Sunday School was a natural pursuit on Sunday, prizes were presented for regular attendance and singing in the choir. The big day was

Harby through the ages

the Sunday School treat when a barge took the children along the canal from Langar Bridge to eventually take tea with the Vicar of Bottesford on the Rectory lawn. 'Parson Stone', a great and much loved man - a 'one off'.

Another early recollection of my Mother's was the return from the Boer War of 'Billy' Cumberland. Nether Street was strung with flags and bunting to welcome him home, this would be around 1902-3.

The Dancing Bear that visited Harby around this time caused much alarm. The Rector was sent for to deal with this situation. The Bear was tied to a gate somewhere near Hose Lane, whilst the owners went to fetch some stale buns or what-ever from the village bake-house. The general feeling was they were 'spies from Russia' - so there you are - nothing changes!!!

The first shop in Nether Street was opened by two ladies in their front room to sell vital necessities to the men digging out the canal, items such as bacon and tobacco twist being the most in demand. The shop in Nether Street was at one time run by my Uncle Joe Musson when he came home from the Great War.

Our great-aunt Matilda Musson was the head-mistress at Harby School. She was a Miss Loder before she married great uncle Sam, hence the name 'Loder Cottage' given to the house where she lived, this house stands back from the Main Street, before you get to the Croft, and the White Hart. There were no badly behaved children in school in those days! Great-aunt Matilda wore a heavy thimble on her finger, and would give a naughty child some 'thimble pie'.

Winters must have been pretty cold around the beginning of the century. On two occasions the canal froze so hard that some young men for a 'dare' took a pony and trap on the canal from Langar to Colston Bridge. The pony had sacking tied around his hooves. Apparently the ice held.

From left to right Dorothy Cooper, Amy Musson, Dorothy's sister Betty Cooper later Holyland in their garden in Harby about 1944. BHOL.

Harby through the ages

The Brewery was a very busy place at Langar Bridge. The building at the right hand side of Langar Bridge was the office for the Brewery. Large Brewery drays pulled by at least four Shires would take casks of ale to be delivered, and some went down the canal in barges. If you wanted a lift to Waltham or the Eastwell cross-roads it was often possible to get a lift on one of these drays if you wished to visit relations further afield. Harby Hill in those days was much steeper than it is now.

I fondly remember the cricket field and hut in Furmidge's field near the Church. It is a great shame this has now gone. We as children in the 1930s used to take a swing down to this field and our Dad used to throw the ropes over the low hanging bough of a tree - the happy hours we had swinging in this field.

There was also a natural spring rising from the ground on the right hand side of the hill in front of Harby woods. Down Langar Lane the fields seemed to be full of cow-slips. I can well imagine the children in my mother's time picking pillow-cases full of cowslips to make the very mellow wine which was so popular. Gleaning was another task which women and children gave much time and energy to. Most country folk had chickens, and this was one way to help feed them.

Just around the corner from the Blacksmiths Forge on the corner of School Lane, (the Forge now sadly gone) was a tiny cottage - once thatched - in which lived an old lady named Jane Wesson. She was quite poor, and when property and land was being sold off after the turn of the century the asking price for Jane's cottage was £50! She just had not got the money to buy it. A local girl who was working in London for a Major Peel and his wife had received this news from home - Major Peel was deeply sorry for this lady, and in a very generous gesture paid for the cottage so she could keep her independence. Jane gave Major Peel a clock in return. Mrs. Peel was a Miss Skinner before she married: of the Lilley and Skinner family in London.

"Dove Cottage" in Dickmans Lane where I lived before moving to my present home, was at one time a Dame School, i.e. a private school. The brick building which adjoins Dove Cottage and now belongs to Harby House was originally the school room. When I purchased Dove Cottage I was amazed to find the original deeds were still with the more up to date deeds. It had quite a history and had at one time been purchased by the Church in hope of a forth-coming marriage between one of the clergy's relations and a certain young lady. However this marriage did not materialise and the property was resold. It then became a Dame School, in 1796. As you probably already know Harby House was built for the use of the two Curates of the Parish, which gives some idea of the power of the church at this time.

Mrs Gibbs, John Mackley's grandmother, had a Shetland pony named 'Dot'. It lived to a ripe 50 years plus and when she died made the news as 'the oldest pony in the World'. Her bones rested in the Royal Veterinary College, in London until they were lost in bombing in World War II.

A small circus came to the village every year until 1966, comprising of just two performers - I later learned they were mother and son. The field they used was at the top of Colston Lane, which contained the telephone exchange. It was not a great variety act - the young man did lasso tricks, and the lady although not young walked the tight-rope!

'Helena' on Waltham Lane where I now live was at one time a small-holding, built in 1919-20. I have known it all my life, and can remember when there were no other buildings between Helena and Starbuck Cottage, and no houses at all down the Main Street until you came to Loder Cottage, The Croft, and the White Hart on the left hand side and the Chapel and the Nag's Head on the right hand side.

It is difficult to imagine just how much every day life has changed since 100 years ago. Life was pretty hard for many folks. Some men were glad to collect churns of water from the canal for a few pence to fill the coppers for women to do their washing on a Monday. One also knew when the 'slop-cart' man was doing his very necessary round. Hedge cuttings were kept to be laid in the deep muddy 'runnels' in Nether Street to help wheels to move more easily when the road was muddy.

1941 DESCRIPTION OF HARBY
Kelly from " Directory of the Counties of Leicestershire and Rutland" page 94.

HARBY is a large village and ecclesiastical parish on the borders of Nottinghamshire, on the south side of the Grantham Canal, with a station called "Harby and Stathern," which is the junction of the Grantham and Melton Mowbray and Melton and Nottingham joint lines of the London and North Eastern and London, Midland and Scottish railways, 1¼ miles south-east of the village, 8¾ north from Melton Mowbray and 14 south-east from Nottingham, in the Melton division of the county, hundred of Framland, petty sessional division of Belvoir, county court district of Melton Mowbray, rural deanery of Framland (first portion), archdeaconry and diocese of Leicester. The church of St. Mary is a building of stone in the Perpendicular style, consisting of chancel, clerestoried nave of three bays, aisles, south porch and an embattled western tower with pinnacles, containing a clock, presented by the Duke of St. Albans, and 5 bells, two dated 1610, one 1614, one 1701 and the fifth 1887: the chancel retains an aumbry and a piscina, and there is also a piscina in the south aisle: the font bears the date 1606: the church was restored and new roofed in 1870, and further restoration took place during 1874 and 1876: a new vestry and organ chamber were added in 1903: there are 220 sittings. The register dates from the year 1700. The living is a rectory, net yearly value £700, including 1 acre of glebe, with residence, in the gift of the Duke of Rutland, and held since 1925 by the Rev. Arthur Evelyn Furnival M.A. of Exeter College, Oxford, rural dean of Framland 1. In the churchyard there was an ancient stone cross, now removed to the village green and reconstructed as a memorial to the men of Harby who fell in the Great War, 1914-18. There is a Methodist chapel, built in 1847. In 1739 the Rev John Major left £10, the interest for the poor of this parish, who also receive £6 13s. 4d.

Watsons Lane about 1940. Miss Ciss Watchorn standing at the front of her house. BTOW..

yearly from Chester's Charity, of Barkstone; Mrs. Hannah Thompson left £10 for the benefit of the church Sunday school in 1866; Mrs. Orson left £20; the Duke of St. Albans gave £40 in 1839: the interest of the above sums, which are all in the care of the Charity Commissioners, is distributed yearly by the rector and Parish Council trustees. The principal landowners are Mrs C. M. Gibbs and Mr George Barke. Electricity is available. Water is supplied by the Melton Rural District Council. The soil is clay; subsoil, clay. The chief crops are beans and wheat and some land in pasture. The population in 1931 was 608.

By the Melton and Belvoir Rural District (Union of Parishes) Order, 1936, this parish was amalgamated with Long Clawson to form the new civil parish of Clawson and Harby.

Post, M. O. & T. Office. Letters through Melton Mowbray
Railway Station (L. & N. E. & L. M. & S)
Conveyance.— Barton Transport Ltd. run an omnibus service to Melton & to Nottingham, daily

Harby through the ages

PRIVATE RESIDENTS.

Booth Mrs
Furnival Rev. Arthur Evelyn M.A. (rector, and rural dean of Framland), Rectory
Watchorn Mrs
Watson Herbt
Wright Harold, The Nook

COMMERCIAL

Marked thus ° farm 150 acres or over.

°Barke Geo. farmer and land owner
Barrett Geo, Hy. insur. agt
Clarke Rd. haulage contrctr
Coy Dan, plumber
Coy Wm, coal mer. TN 216
Dewey Jas. Akerman, butcher
Dickman & Woolley, millers (oil engine), The Mill. TN 210
Dickman Thomas, bldr. TN 232
°Furmidge Harry, farmer. TN 266
Gale Bernard, grazier
°Gibbs C. Marion (Mrs.), farmer & landowner. TN 221
Harby Farmers' Dairy Ltd. (The), cheese mkrs
Haywood John, grazier
Heywood Harry, farmer, Hills farm
Kemp Eustace, grazier
Kemp R. E. (Mrs.), grazier
Lamin Jn. Edwd. grazier
Mackley Wm. T. cycle agt. TN 222
Martin Ernest, wheelwright
Mawson Lillian Ann (Mrs.), grazier, Lillydene
Nag's Head P. H. (Austin F. Price). TN 209
National Deposit (Approved) Friend Society (Jn. Stroud, sec)
Pepper Fredk. grocer, & Post office. TN 200
Pepper Thomas Wm. Grazier
Pick J. J. & W, farmers
Pickard Eliz. Ann (Mrs.), poultry farmer
Pickard Jsph. grazier
°Rawlinson Annie (Mrs.), farmer
Rawlinson Ernest, farmer
Starbuck Saml. & Son, motor engnrs. TN 213
Stead Mabel (Mrs.), shopkpr
Stead Martin, blacksmith
Stokes Thos. plumber & glazier
Swingler Jesse, farmer, Harby lodge
United Dairies (Wholesale) Ltd. cheese mkrs. TN 208
°Walker A. & C. farmers
Watchorn T. Wm. grazier
White Hart P. H. (Mark M Curtis). TN 237
White Joseph farmer
Wiles T. W. G. grazier
Wilford James Corner, farmer

MEMORIES OF HARBY 1944 to 1963 *Wendy Starbuck*

When I was 7, June Kemp and I went to Woody Butcher's at lunchtime to have her warts charmed away. Woody looked at the warts and gave us tea and bread and butter and we waited and waited for her to say the magic spells and put her pointed hat on. She didn't and we were late back to school. She hadn't done anything! The warts disappeared.

Woody and her brother lived in School Lane opposite the Institute. She had an enormous goitre which greatly enhanced her image as the 'wise woman'. My mum said she could charm warts and help animals to get better. She was a kindly lady who gave me my first houseplant. It died. I obviously didn't have her powers.

There were two distinct territories in the village – the Top End and the Bottom End. We Bottom End kids were a bit scared of the Top Enders. Once, when we got chased by Top End boys, they stuffed maggots and a dead starling down our backs. I've had a horror of dead birds ever since!

In the summer we children would go haymaking at Furmidge's Farm next to the church. A bottle of Vimto was essential. We would all ride in the big wooden hay wagon behind the tractor and sing on the way to the hayfield. You had to walk back or (if you were lucky and didn't mind the teasing) you might get a ride on a boy's bike crossbar.

Miss Buxton would give you a penny if you ran an errand to the post office for her. She was our infant teacher. We liked her very much. I remember her twin sets and pearls and comforting bosom. Looking back I realise what an excellent teacher she was and how much she loved us kids. A penny at the post office would buy two ha'penny chews, a traffic light gob stopper, 4 liquorice laces, a sherbert sucker, or a quarter of 'rat turds' (pronounced 'tods'). I think they are more delicately called 'liquorice torpedoes' now.

Mr. Lane was the headmaster at Harby School in the fifties. He was a truly inspirational teacher and made going to school interesting. We listened to Schools radio, went on nature walks to the canal, worked out the area of the playground. He let me paint the sky green the same as in the print of Van Gogh's caravans which hung in the classroom. We had awful mental arithmetic tests in the afternoons and I was caught cheating.

There was a tennis court in the rectory garden and village people were allowed to use it. The tennis balls were kept in a brick hovel but it was guarded by a flock of rectory geese. If you wanted to play you had to risk the wrath of God's geese. We'd go scrumping in Bastick's orchard and Boyer's orchard (it was a real orchard then). Someone would yell, 'Blundy's coming!' We'd go pelting down the road, hearts thumping, raining apples. P.C. Blundy was a man of swift and summary justice.

Harby school May 1954 taken in the field to the west of the church. From left to right :- Back row – Diane White, Christine Moulds, Anthea Pritchett, Jennifer Waring, Eric Lane, Thelma Rawlings, Margaret Slater, Marion Mackley, Valerie Herrick. Middle row – Pam Kemp, June Bremner, Valerie Leon, Wendy Starbuck, Pauline Wright, Josie Derby, Julia Brown, Mary Rawlings, Carol Tinsley. Front row – Ian Slater, Colin Moulds, Tommy Wilson, Sam Towers. BTOW.

There were two Nelly Starbucks in the village. One was my mum, the other lived by the post office and had a Jack Russell terrier.

Opposite my dad's garage were the blacksmith's shop and a tiny white cottage on the opposite side of the junction. Miss Kemp lived there. The grassy corner next to her house was known as Parliament Corner because all the old chaps used to congregate there in the evenings and put the world to rights. There was a large, very distinctive stone on that corner. It seems to have disappeared.

When I was 15 or 16 I was seen kissing a boy from Clawson at the bus stop. Someone told the Rector in the post office. The Rector told my mum. Mum said that if I wasn't careful I would 'get a reputation'. A 'reputation' was dire indeed in Harby in the Fifties and early Sixties.

I was adopted and it wasn't a secret, though in the Forties and Fifties it was considered rather shameful. No-one in the village, not even the children, ever said anything unkind to me. I was very lucky to grow up in Harby. My mum and dad, Harry and Nelly Starbuck, were wonderful parents.

*School Lane looking up to the school, from Nether Street about 1968.
Mrs Butcher lived in the white house on the right side. People went to her to have their warts charmed away. She would take the part of the body afflicted with them and count them as she pointed to them, "One, two, three, etc".
LCRA*

1952 MAP

This is the Ordnance Survey map of the village in 1952 at the scale of 1:10,560, (6 inches to 1 mile), SK73 SW and SK 73 SE. Along the north side of School Lane and at the east of the village on the north of Stathern Lane semi-detached "council houses" have been built by Melton and Belvoir Rural District Council in 1936 to 1937 and rented out. Around 1947 there has been further council house building on Pinfold Place to the north of the Stathern Lane council houses. There are new allotment gardens next to the Pinfold Place council houses off Stathern Lane. There are also a few new private dwellings on Langar Lane. For those who can afford them there are modern services available, telephone, electricity, mains water, and sewerage. For the houses in Langar Lane the sewage discharged untreated into the canal at Langar Bridge.

Harby through the ages

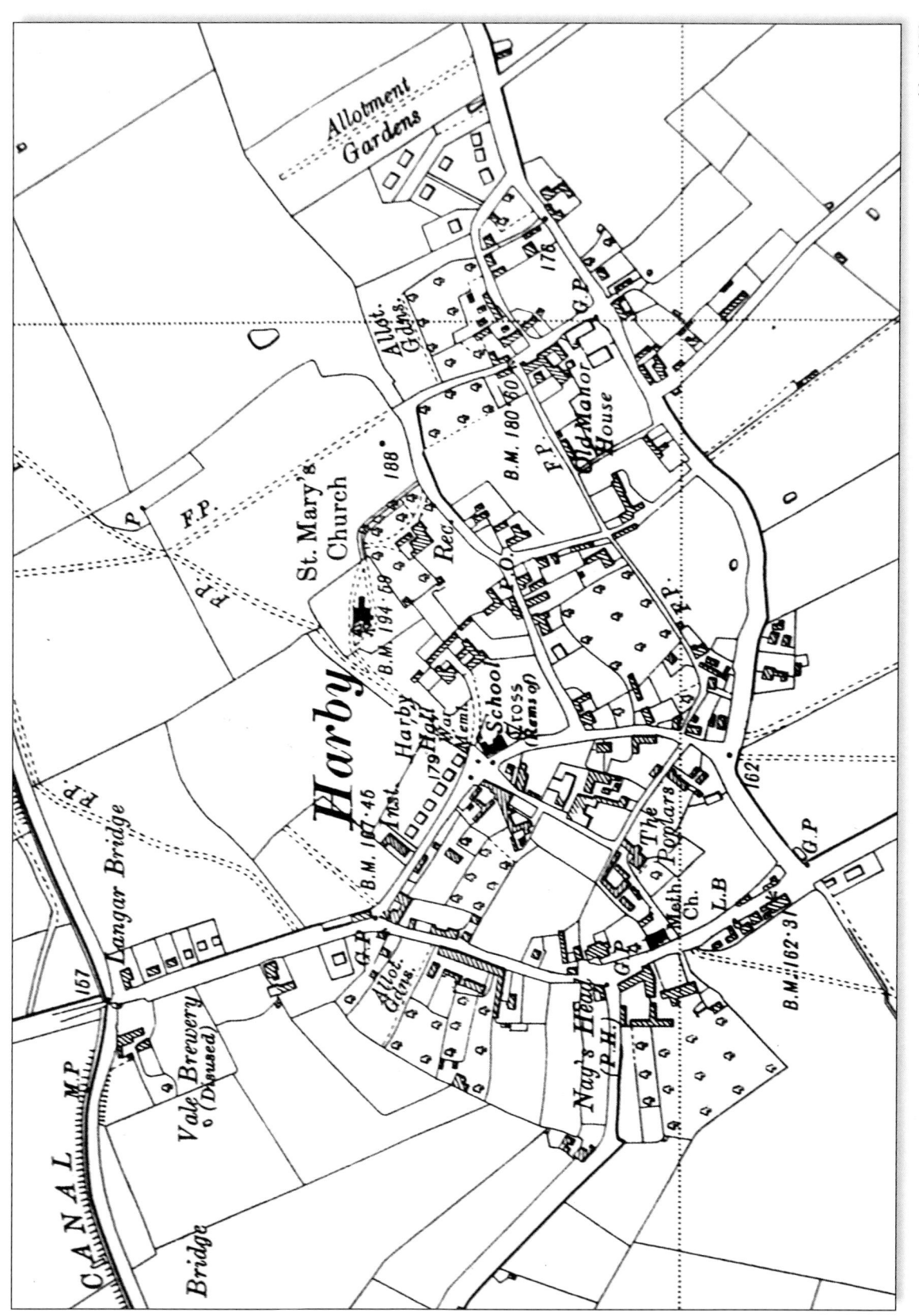

Map 1952

Harby: Village life in the Vale of Belvoir

Harby through the ages
MEMORIES FROM 1944 TO 1975 *Tom Sadler*

When I first came to the village in 1944 it was a rural farming area in the true sense of the word. Near the canal bridge on Langar Lane was Brian Wilford's farm, now a barn conversion unit. Near the Public Houses, the Nag's Head and the White Hart, was the Muxloe's farm. Just along Colston Lane was Les Shipman's farm. Along Stathern Lane was George Dewey's farm, and farther on the Walker's farm. Opposite Pinfold Place was "Pudding" Whittaker's small farm and right in the middle of the village opposite the old Post office premises was Bill Pepper's farm, and more or less behind that was the Furmidge's farm. In Pinfold Lane was Buck Watchorn's farm, and I used to collect milk from there for one or two people, each day straight from the churn! It was good milk and seemed to have no ill-effect on anyone! Cows in and around the village were very much a part of everyday life as they were brought in for milking and then returned to their fields. There was of course a certain amount of "fouling" of the road, but it was all part and parcel of country life. As the changes began to occur people from the urban areas were moving out into the country villages, and some years later, when I was a Parish Councillor I remember a "new-comer" making a complaint about the fouling at a Parish Meeting, and being asked by a farming Councillor "What would you have us do, fit them all with napkins? If you want to live among us then you will have to live the way we do!" It was a "bone of contention" at that time when people were moving away from the urban areas, and then seemed hell-bent on bringing urbanisation with them to the country areas! To a certain extent they have succeeded if you compare the village of today with the way it used to be!

When I first came to Harby there were no new houses. World War II had put a stop to most domestic building and the village was distinctly pre-war in appearance. Mains water and electricity were not facilities enjoyed by everyone and cooking in the majority of cottages was done on old-fashioned grates with a side oven and a small water tank to one side or on three-burner paraffin stoves specially designed for the purpose. The small built-in tank at the side of the fire grate provided a small amount of hot water by way of a tap on the front of the actual boiler. Bathrooms were not as we know them today and were only for the better-off households and even then were primitive compared with the standard we expect today. Most families had a tin bath and bathing was usually done on one day each week usually in front of the living room fire! In the absence of electricity lighting in the majority of ordinary homes was by way of paraffin lamps. Running water was available if you could afford to have it laid on, and consisted of a cold tap only. The majority of the houses relied on a hand pump in the yard which pumped water directly from a well in the ground. Sometimes one pump had to serve several households. Most of the old cottages had a fire-heated copper in which the family washing was done on a weekly basis. This usually took place on Mondays. The copper had to be filled with water, either from a pump, or if it was connected, a cold tap from the water main. The fire was then lit under the copper and, as the water boiled, in went the family washing. Then, using a separate wash-tub, into which boiling water and soapflakes were put, and using a "Paunch" and "Dolly", the clothes were "churned"

Harby through the ages

Coming back from school in 1946. The view is from near Stathern Lane looking up to the school in the distance. From left to right are in the front - Herbert Fairbrother with his granddaughter Sheila Fairbrother; behind - Eileen Fairbrother, Ruth Fairbrother (twin of Sheila), Freda Fairbrother. FBAN.

Boyers Orchard with apple blossom around 1950. This is at the north end looking over the road to the gate into the Wong field. The houses on the west side of Boyers Orchard leading down to Stathern Lane were first occupied from May 1956. BCLA.

Inside the cottage next to Dickman's cottage in Dickmans Lane in 1950. Mr Reeves with a candle to light him to bed. Mr. Reeves' cottage was not equipped with electricity. He had lived in Harby for 60 years. The rent of the cottage, 3s. 3d. per week, had not changed for 25 years. The cottage used to be two homes. From The Illustrated Leicester Chronicle of August 19 1950, page 10.

Harby: Village life in the Vale of Belvoir

Harby through the ages

manually to clean them. Blue dye was added to the water to give extra sparkle to the "whites" and the operation was repeated over and over again until all the family wash was done. Each lot was then rinsed in clean water and put through a "mangle" to squeeze out the excess water. Depending on the amount of washing to be done, the term "washday" was just that. It was hard work for the lady of the house, and then remember all of it had to be dried, outside if the weather was favourable, or inside around the fire on a "clothes horse" if not. Then came the ironing using old-fashioned flat irons heated on the fire. The copper also served to heat the water used on "bathday", often having to be boiled several times to cater for families. Coal was the fuel used on the fires and there were local coal merchants who made weekly deliveries to each household. Harby was served in the main by W. Coy and Son and the descendants still live locally. As electricity became available to all the use of electric irons and heaters became the order of the day and made life considerably less taxing. Washing machines were to follow and a woman's life became a comparative "doddle" compared to their old time counterparts.

Carpets were a luxury and the majority of floors at that time were either tiles, which had to be scrubbed by hand, or linoleum, with the odd rug, many home-made, to alleviate the shock of stepping out of bed onto cold linoleum! That gives a little insight into the way people lived in the early post-World War II days of the 50s and early 60s.

Stathern Lane was prone to pretty severe flooding and the old sewerage system discharged into the ditch behind the fairly modern houses that now stand at the bottom of Waltham Lane, opposite the exit from Stathern Lane. It was quite inadequate and in the 60s was replaced by the system which is in operation today. It served also to alleviate the flood problem.

The Poplars paddock in the 1960s, looking along Main Street to the junction with Stathern Lane and Waltham Road. On the platform are the churns of milk waiting to be collected, a common sight around Harby at this time. JWAT.

Boyers Orchard in the 1960s, on the way to the church Flower Service usually held on the first Sunday in July. The girl with basket at the front is Sarah Blundy, the three girls behind are from left to right, Wendy Whittle, possibly Anne Blundy and Susan Townsend. The gate to the allotments is just behind them. An old pantechnicon body, coloured maroon is in Mackley's Orchard on the left. The car rear wing is of a 1950 Hillman Minx. Girls often had a new dress each year for the Flower Service. Bunches of flowers were taken into church for the service. After the service the congregation would come into the church yard and encircle the church while they sang a hymn. This was known as "clipping the church". The flowers were then left on the graves of relatives. JBLU.

The village had its own policeman in the person of Harry Blundy, a well built, no-nonsense sort of man who could be relied upon to deal with most of the problems concerning law and order in his own inimitable way! He was a much-respected figure and one that you didn't particularly want to be at cross-purposes with! As I have said, he had his own methods and maintained law and order using a bicycle as his means of transport to serve and police three or four surrounding villages! I've seen him throw two airmen at once out of the village hall for misbehaving themselves holding them one in each hand, by the scruff of their necks. You didn't mess with Harry! He eventually retired and since his time there have been two further policemen each living in the one-time police house opposite the Dewey's old farm. There is no village policeman now. Harry's descendants still live in the village.

The village "hops" were well attended by the airmen from Langar who were quite popular with the local ladies! The entrance fee was 6 pence in old money, 2 ½ pence in today's coinage, and the music could be anything from a "radiogram" to a piano and drums, and maybe an accordion. A very strong community spirit existed and the various little groups of people organised local entertainment which in the main was well patronised. Refreshments were prepared and donated by the ladies, which added to the profit. There were practically no cars in private ownership but the Barton Bus Company, who had a parking depot in the village on Stathern Lane, ran buses to Melton Mowbray and Nottingham which enabled people to travel for extra entertainment and shopping trips. The main employment was either, (1) at Harby Dairy, run by the Watson family, which was situated opposite the end of Burden Lane on School Lane, (2) the aircraft company A V Roe, in the buildings opposite the airfield at Langar, or (3) the REME depot at Old Dalby. All the above closed as the years went by. There were also those who worked elsewhere of course and who used bicycle or bus transport to travel to and fro.

Harby through the ages

The village boasted a quite successful football team, and a very successful cricket team with a cricket square situated in the field behind the village hall which was generally regarded as above average standard for a village. The football team produced quality players who were in fact "scouted" by professional clubs!

The local Post Office and general store was situated at the northern end of Dickmans Lane, and was run by Mr Pepper, (no relation to the farmer as far as I am aware), who was known locally as "The Duke". The post office counter was situated just inside the main door to the premises on the left, and I can still visualise the well-built figure of the "Duke" behind the counter with a stub of cigarette dangling from his tobacco stained lips! He had an efficient and industrious assistant in the person of Miss Hallam who ran the shop, assisted later on by Doreen Moulds, a local girl. She became the mainstay when Miss Hallam retired. The son was Jack Pepper who in later years took over and at one time started a mink breeding venture, behind the post office which eventually caused a minor scare when it was alleged one of the mink had escaped and was on the loose! I know not how that ended! There is an interesting story concerning the Post Office and Royalty. It seems that a member of the Royal Family had been hunting with one of the local hunts and for some reason took a bath at the Post Office. The bar of soap he used was preserved by the Pepper family as memorabilia and I am left wondering where that bar of soap is now - always assuming it is still in existence! When I finally came back and settled in Harby in the early 1960s there were also two other shops in the village at that time. Mrs Holland kept the general shop in the cottage opposite the "Cross" near the school, and Brent Harriman kept another general store on Nether Street opposite the end of what is now Burton Close. They all seemed satisfied just to serve the village and make a modest living rather than a quick fortune!

At the south end of Green Lane with Rutland Terrace in the distance, about 1955, from left to right are Gladys Looms nee Cunnington, Doris Cunnington and Alice Hodges (nee Cunnington). NCUN.

Harby through the ages

Like every other village I guess Harby had its share of "characters". The most notable that I can remember was a somewhat odd chap who wore a shoulder brace-strap arrangement and lived locally with his wife, who could be equally eccentric! This man used to crow like a cockerel on his way home in the dark along Stathern Lane, and could be heard all over the area! Whilst Harby was not subjected to actual enemy bombing the locals were only too aware of the war as the planes took off and landed by day and night on Langar Airfield, particularly at the time No 207 Squadron were operational from there, going almost daily to bomb enemy territory, many of the crews never to return.

As the years moved on, more and more of the old faces disappeared and more and more of the old cottages gave way to new dwellings. Inevitably the village atmosphere began to change to accommodate the new ideas. Most of the old population had grown up together as families, and some had inter-married, and people knew most of what there was to know about each other. With the introduction of newcomers, of which I was one, less and less was known of the history and relationships and the way of life changed. I wonder in years to come will the newer groups of people have established themselves in the same intertwined way and at some time in the future will someone else be attempting to write a record of their memories as I am now doing? I suppose the answer is, "Of course they will, each generation has their own values and memories and they are just as important to them as mine are to me".

Harby in winter, perhaps the hard winter of 1947, looking from the back of Sherbooke House on Colston Lane to Main Street with the church tower in the distance at the centre. JWAT.

Nether Street about 1947, from the south looking towards School Lane, with Harriman's store on the left. JWAT.

Harby: Village life in the Vale of Belvoir

Harby through the ages

A very memorable period followed in the 60s and 70s when a group of enthusiastic villagers decided that the social life in the village was in need of some new ideas. The driving force was the man who was at that time the village policeman, P.C. Peter Handley. He suggested that a meeting be called inviting villagers to attend, which was subsequently arranged to take place in the Village School, courtesy of the then Headmaster, who made no charge, with a view to forming a new group to deal with village entertainment. The Village Institute Committee, which had kept things running in their own way, were an ageing body of people, and rather than trying to change their ways, it was felt that the easiest way would be a separate organisation whose sole interest would be to promote entertainment more suited to the post-war community. We duly met, and 15 to 20 people turned up. Peter Handley took the chair and the result was that the Harby Community Association (later known as the HCA) was formed, and all those who attended agreed to become Committee members! It may seem like an unwieldy number of people, but in fact it worked well. We had no money, but at that meeting it was arranged that we put on our first dance in the Village Institute, and that between us we would finance it without remuneration and any profit would be the starting point of an HCA bank account. We were a tiny bit worried that it would not succeed. We hired the Village Institute and, with their co-operation, the week or so before the dance took place we all assembled each evening in the Institute and set about transforming the interior to match the theme of the dance. My memory fails me at this point and I cannot remember what that first theme was. It may well have been "Easter Bonnet". The committee provided all the materials for the transformation and the response was tremendous, as word got round about the trouble we were taking. We made a profit and never looked back. We agreed that probably 3 or 4 per year on the same lavish scale would be enough and each one would coincide with a particular occasion, i.e. Easter, Harvest Festival, Halloween, Christmas, Valentine's Day etc. oh yes, and a Tramps Supper. Hilarious. We were particularly fortunate to have among us at that time various people who would either supply free of charge or at discount price, the sort of materials required to transform the interior of the Institute, as it was then called, and the enthusiasm of the committee ensured that the labour was there to carry it out. Entrance was by ticket only, priced at a very low level, but one which the committee felt was within comfortable reach of everyone, to be sold by committee members only, so that there was some check on who were in attendance. Yes, there were disruptive elements in those days also! Each function without exception was a complete sell out. This did become embarrassing at times as word of mouth spread farther afield and tickets were sold out before local residents had obtained theirs. The number of tickets available was governed by the legal limit to the number of people allowed in the Institute at any one time and a local publicised deadline had to be set before tickets became widely available to the general public, to ensure that locals got "first crack of the whip". All the refreshments were donated by the committee members and their friends, and it should be noted that there was no "bar" allowed. It didn't seem necessary in those days, although the rules of the Institute were later changed relaxing the consumption of alcohol on the premises. The HCA continued for a number of years, but, as is the case with so many organisations, the ageing process of the driving forces saw its demise and it was wound up. The money accumulated in the bank account was handed over to the Institute Committee and a few of us transferred our allegiance to that committee, taking a few new ideas with us. As Bob Watson, a former well respected member of the local community, and long serving Manager of Wilts. Dairy, once said to me, "If you drew a graph of village life you would find that it showed highs and lows of most things in a 5 year cycle". I think he was not too far from the truth.

Dickmans Lane in 1950, looking south with Dickman's Cottage in the far right, and Mr Dickman walking towards the camera. The Lane was named after his grandfather. The house opposite Dickman's cottage used to be the Dame School. From The Illustrated Leicester Chronicle of August 19, 1950, page 10.

1971 MAP

The village as shown on the Ordnance Survey 1:2,500 scale, 25 miles to one inch, map of 1971 (Leicestershire 7431). It is from the 1971 Ordnance Survey map reproduced by permission of Ordnance Survey on behalf of HMSO.© Crown Copyright 1971. All rights reserved. Ordnance Survey Licence number 100050271. It shows extensive house building since the 1952 map. Looking at the map from west to east, left to right, on the other side of Nether Street from Exchange Row, the new Burton Close has some dozen detached private dwellings built about 1970. The triangle of land between Stathern Lane and Main Street is now infilled with housing; private dwellings erected about 1965 on Main Street and Stathern Lane in what was the paddock to the Poplars and council bungalows built about 1969 along Watsons Lane. Private houses have gone up along the east side of Dickmans Lane. Council houses have been built about 1959 on the extension of Boyers Orchard opposite the rectory. About 1956 council houses had already been built on the west side of Boyers Orchard as the road turns down towards Stathern Lane. There are new private dwellings at the south end of Green Lane. The only working farms still situated within the built-up area of the village are Manor Farm at the south end of Boyers Orchard and Sherbrooke Farm on Colston Lane. The Old Rectory has been sold and a smaller new one built on the west of the grounds. The graveyard of the Parish Church has been extended to the east. This in fact happened in 1943/44 but for some reason is not shown on the 1952 map. The stone wall which separates the churchyard from the Old Rectory on the south originally extended along the east side and was taken down to make the extension. The earliest burial in the extension is dated 1944.

Harby through the ages

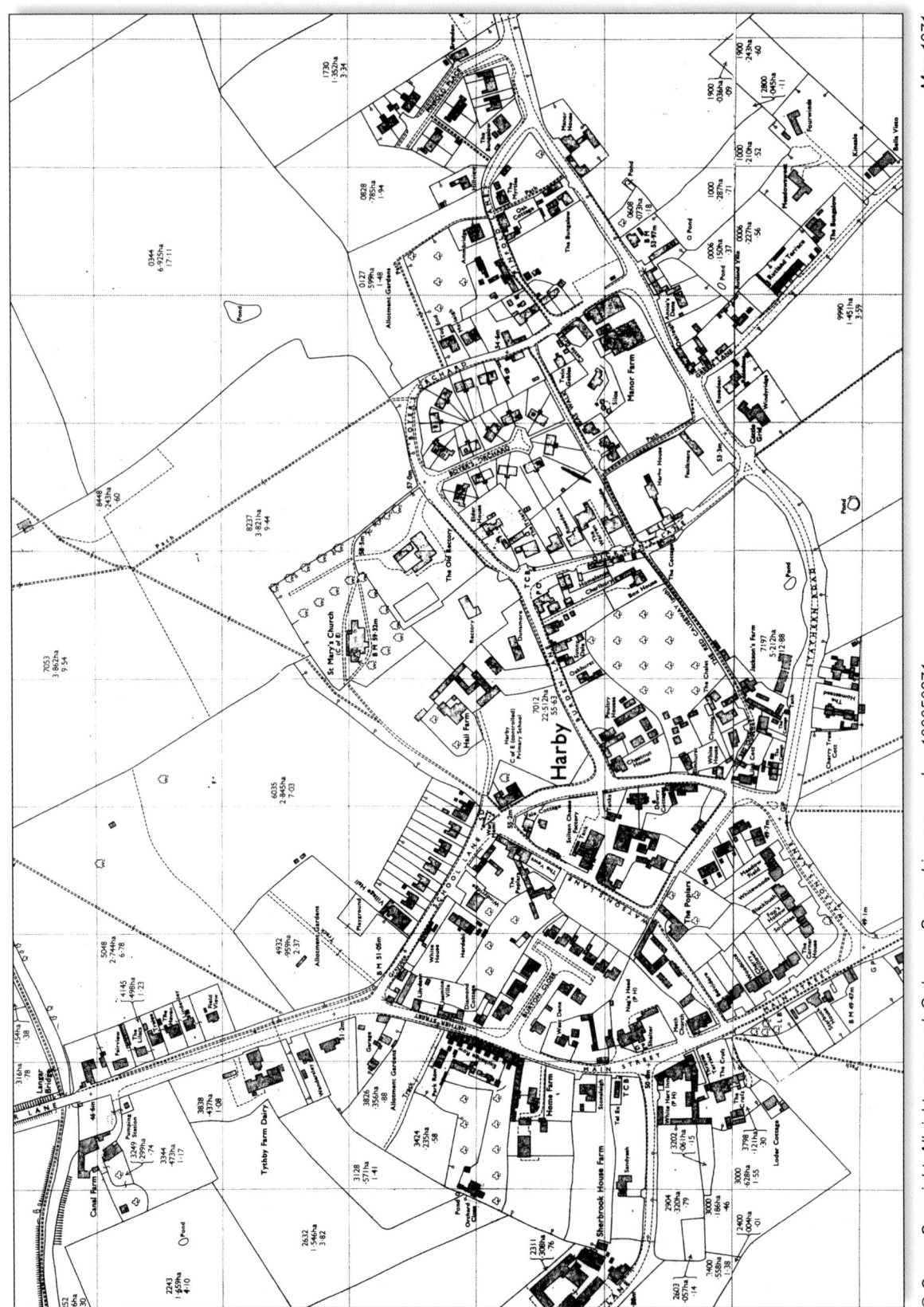

Map 1971

© Crown Copyright. All rights reserved. Ordnance Survey Licence number 100050271

ASPECTS OF HARBY LIFE

1. HARBY AT WORK
BLACKSMITH AND BUILDING
THE DIARIES OF MARTIN STEAD - VILLAGE BLACKSMITH
Rex Stapleford

Martin Sunderland Stead was born in 1876 at Radford in Nottinghamshire. His father was a wheelwright. Martin went into the related business of blacksmithing. While working at Long Clawson he lived in Harby where he met Mabel (nicknamed Bab) Furmidge. They were married in 1907 and Martin set up in business with William Swingler, with forges at Stathern and at the west end of School Lane in Harby. The couple initially lived in Horseshoe Cottage opposite the school. They had two children, Barbara and Martin. Martin's father had a wheelwright business in Carlton, Nottingham at this time and his brother Frank lived near Nottingham. Martin's wife's sister was Grace and Jack Stanyon her husband. During the First World War Martin made horseshoes for the government. The business prospered and he bought land in Burden Lane and had his own house, Oakhurst, built in 1930. He died in 1963.

Martin Sunderland Stead the blacksmith at his anvil, from Illustrated Leicester Chronicle 9 October 1937 page 5.

Four volumes of diaries kept by Martin Stead were acquired by John Billings. They cover the years 1915 and then 1922 to January 1931. There is usually an entry for each day. Selections are summarized and transcribed below. The year 1915 has summaries. The later years of 1922 to 1930 have transcriptions. They are published here with the generous agreement of John Billings.

Martin Stead's forge in 1937, on the corner of School Lane and Nether Street, from Illustrated Leicester Chronicle, 9 October 1937, page 5. .

Harby life

1915

January to March

The first entry in the 1915 diary relates to a parcel that got lost in the post. It is a draft of a letter to the post office, requesting a settlement of a claim for 15 shillings. Martin states that he has proof of posting at Harby Post Office on the 23rd of December 1914 at 4.30pm, that can be verified by Mrs J Watchorn at the post office. From the 2nd to the 4th of January he was in bed with influenza, but on Tuesday the 5th he started work at midday following delivery of iron. On Friday the 8th he commenced making government horseshoes.

By the end of January he had dispatched five hundredweight of government shoes. By the end of March he had despatched a further 18 cwt of shoes. The total amount of government cheques he received for three months work amounted to just over £40. In addition to his government work, Martin was still providing a service to local farmers, for example, on Tuesday, the 2nd of February, he was shoeing eight young horses at Hubbard's Farm at Langar.

May

On Friday, the 7th of May SS Lusitania was torpedoed and on Tuesday the 18th of May the news came of the deaths of Mabbott and Hoyes in France. On Monday the 31st of May, 30 soldiers of the 22nd Section of the 8th Battalion, machinegun section of the Manchester Regiment were billeted in the new schoolroom.

June - July

On Friday the 4th of June he sat the 'black hen' on 10 bantam and 5 hen eggs. The Royal show was on at Nottingham on the 29th and 30th of June. He took Martin Samuel on his bike to his parents home at Carlton on Sunday the 18th of July and on Tuesday the 27th he had news of cousin Arthur's wedding.

August

Jack and Grace came on the 2nd of August Bank Holiday Monday, and there was a tennis tournament on the same day. On Thursday the 12th of August, J Swingler's boy broke his thigh, and in the evening the Rev G Oyston preached and lectured at night. Cycled to Nottingham to see J Swingler on the 28th, Saturday.

September

On Wednesday the 8th of September, his father and Arthur came for half a day, and they went to Belvoir. They returned to Nottingham on the last train. Martin went to Nottingham on the first train on Saturday the 11th of September and bought a pony from Netherfield. He stopped overnight at Carlton. That morning he had received a letter from the Director of Army contracts with reference to more horseshoes. He left Carlton the next morning at 6 am with pony and arrived home at about 11.30am. Oliver Swingler died on Sunday the 12th of September and the funeral was on the 14th. The contract for more Army shoes was received on Wednesday the 15th, and on the 17th he bought 3 black pigs from J Stokes for £3.17s.0d. Feast Sunday was on the 26th and

Harby life

the following day there was a flower show. Nurse Welsh and Kit came for tea and Barbara won first prize in the fancy dress parade dressed as a nurse.

November, December

On Tuesday November 16th, Elsie Kemp's fiance came to Harby and stayed with us overnight. Babs went to the Rawlinson's whist drive on the 19th and Mr Peppiatt was due to embark at 4pm. On Thursday the 23rd of December, killed 2 cockerels for Christmas, on the 24th trimmed the Christmas tree. On Christmas day Martin's mam and dad came for tea.

In the yard of Mr Ernie Martin the wheelwright and undertaker on the north side of Stathern Road between Boyers Orchard and Pinfold Lane, perhaps in the late 1940s. The cart is an hermaphrodite, dual purpose type, which converted for muck spreading in the winter, with the name "C Tomlinson Harby" painted on the side. If there was not room for the body to lie in the house until the funeral Ernie woud take a coffin on his hand cart to collect it. BCLA.

1922

Wednesday January 11. Drove to station after tea & fetched bags Stamford horseshoes (7 cwt).

Wednesday January 18. Will went to Eaton to shoe Royal Commander.

Tuesday February 28. Princess Mary married.

Wednesday March 15. Had 7 lbs distemper (mahogany lake) of Dennis & Roberts.

Friday March 17. Sold Bab's porker to R Miller for £4=0=0 (about 6 stones).

Saturday March 18. Hen turkey laid first egg. Bought 10 rolls of paper for big bedroom @ 10 d per roll.

Monday March 27. Whitewashed big bedroom ceiling at night.

Tuesday March 28. Papered bedroom morning.

Wednesday April 5. Sold all litter pigs (17) & old sow to Fairbrother £35=0=0. Snowstorm at night.

Saturday July 22. Motored to Bingham & took Martin & Bab to Doncasters Sale. Bought

Harby life

– cap 2/6d; 1 pr. braces 10½d; 1pr. trousers 10/6d; 1 pr. overalls 8/6d, tie 1/6d.

Saturday October 7th Goose Fair. Rode BSA to Carlton after tea, & went on to fair with Frank, & failed to get start home that night. Stayed & returned Sun. morning. Cousin Arthur was to have come to Carlton but failed to do so.

Saturday December 23. Mam & children went to Coventry by 11 train. Bab & I followed later by 6-30.

Tuesday December 26. All came home by the 4.30 train from Coventry. Reached Harby by last Nottingham train (8), & was met at station with Greaves motor.

1923
Friday June 29. Heard Musson's wire-less & made iron stay pole for same.

Sunday July 22. Loughboro clarillion peal dedicated & memorial unveiled.

1925
Monday May 18. Church struck by lightning.
Saturday September 19. New Institute opened at night for first time. Met Jack & Grace by 5 train. Bab went to Nottingham & took Barbara to buy her coat. Met her with car by 3 train. Very heavy rains.
Sunday September 20. Feast Sunday. Went to church with Jack. New minister preached at chapel. Harvest Festival at church and chapel. Heavy rain storms.
Monday September 21. Flower and poultry show. Wet at intervals. Went to feast at night.
Tuesday December 8. Wrote to Brown Bros about Brownie crystal set.

Wednesday December 9. Fixed aerial pole for wireless.

Thursday December 10. Put wireless earth in front garden & aerial on roof. Sent to Brown Bros for 100 ft wire & Brownie terminal board.

Martin Stead outside his forge in 1937, on the corner of School Lane and Nether Street.

Monday December 14. Brownie wireless set came. Fixed bracket for aerial to chimney.

Tuesday December 15. Fixed aerial & listened in at night.

Thursday December 17. Listened in to Messiah on wireless.

Thursday December 31. Sat up & heard old year out on wireless.

1926
Wednesday May 12. General Strike called off at 1.30pm by Trades Union Council. Martin landed home from school about 9pm.

Saturday, June 12. First Test Match at Trent Bridge (Australians) stopped through rain.

1927
Thursday November 17. Prince of Wales opened the new bridge at Gunthorpe

Sunday November 20. Had run to Gunthorpe to see new bridge with Martin in car.

Tuesday December 27. Foot & Mouth disease spreading in Notts, Derby & Leics. Standstill order issued.

1928
Tuesday January 10. March snowstorms all day & night, sunshine in between. Had lady doctor, & had to stay in with bad cold. Had bottle of medicine. Bab & Barbara went to Choir practice at Clawson for the Messiah.

Monday January 16. Chapel class at night, few there but good meeting, tried new piece 'Medley Glee'. Had load straw from Fairbrother.

Thursday June 28. Garden Fete, went up at 2.30 to serve at gate. Affair spoilt by weather.

Wednesday September 26. Shod two mares & foals at Harwood's for Melton sale.

Friday November 29. Took Barbara & Mrs Manchester to hear National Children's Home Choir at Long Clawson.

Wednesday December 12. Wet day. Met Mr David Griffiths at Melton M R Station at 3.45 pm. Mr Griffiths lectured at 7 on the blind at work & at play. A very fine lecture & good company, 27/6d collected at door, besides the sale of 200 tickets at 6d each. Total proceeds £6 =12s=0.

Thursday December 13. Took Mr Griffiths to Harby station to catch the 3.15pm train to Nottm en-route to Sheffield.

Thursday December 21. Sam Starbuck had electric light on for first time.

December 25. Barbara & I went to morning service at church.

Harby life

December 29 . Altered carburettors on car. Hounds met at Colston Bassett & came through Harby later.

1929

Wednesday January 2. Had New Year's party. Those present; Mr & Mrs T Manchester, Sam & Belle Furmidge, Jack & Roy Faulds (or Faulks), Enid & Queen. Marjorie Furmidge & Eva came about 8 pm. Party broke up at 11.30pm.

Thursday January 3 Cycled to Clawson to see Buxton about old cart tyres (£4 per ton).

Saturday March 9. Took Barbara in s.c. (sidecar) to Old Dalby for weekend. After tea went to Carlton & took Martin.

Tuesday April 9. Went to Melton on Coy's new bus 9-30. Paid Shafto the rent - ordered fire bricks.

Saturday April 27. Tennis started. Putting top wire on court & extending top end of court. Harry Scarboro, Martin & I. Paid T Stokes 2/3d for 9 wire posts for court & 50 yards of wire from T Danks at 19/5.

Tuesday, May 7. Will came. Making cart horse shoes out old tyres. Dan Coy papered Martin's bedroom after tea. I set half home garden with Edwards potatoes. Dibbled them in. Paid N. D. Club to Mr Edwards at the school for the first time.

May 20. Whit Monday. Harry Scarboro & I measured & marked out court first thing. Had tennis tournament all day. Very warm, lovely day, thermometre 99 deg in sun in yard.

Thursday May 23. Chapel anniversary & centenary celebration of Methodism at Harby. Rev Benson Perkins preached & lectured. Lovely day.

Saturday June 15. Splashing lane hedge & finishing chicken run in orchard.

Tuesday June 25. Fetched old tree from H Furmidge. Sawed same with cross cutter. Martin led it home with mare & light cart.

Saturday June 29. Barbara went to Dalby (by bus in Melton). I went over on BSA to see Mr A Brown about car insurance due on July 1st.

Monday, August 12. Went with choir to Leamington, Warwick & Coventry & called at Lutterworth going. Coy's bus & Mackley's car. 24 in all. Had tea at Graces. Fare £6 to which each adult paid 1/6 in bus & 2/- in car. Good day's outing.

Saturday August 31. Tennis tea & friendly match arranged but thunder & rain prevented it. Very close all day & heavy rain storms later. Hot & fine all week: grand harvest weather!

Friday September 12. Addressed Stathern meeting about Guild work. They decided to start a Guild & elected officers same evening.

Wednesday September 18. Tennis supper at our house. Club members all invited. Ladies contributed articles of food & paid 3d, gents paid 6d for their supper. Some played tennis from 5 pm until dusk. Supper at 8 pm, dancing on the lawn. Proceeds 9/-.

Sunday November 10. Wet morning. Got up & took Jowett out for trial spin along Long Lane.

Friday November 29. Fixed railings around the cross.

Saturday November 30. Martin took young sow down to Strouds. Arthur Adams came across & tested car battery. Had a run to Belvoir cross-roads. Dr Saunders lecture at school 6.45 pm.

Thursday December 12. Went to Clawson at night to Messiah choir practice, Bab, Barbara & self. Martin also went.

Wednesday December 25. After a good dinner, Martin & I had a walk as far as Fairbrother's lodge. Eva came about 7.30pm & brought presents, mine was a car licence holder. Very rough wind all day but fine.

1930

Sunday January 5. Went to Frank's & got another headlight bulb 2/9 & called at Carlton & got 2 galls of Shell.

Saturday February 8. Went on Coy's 5.30 bus to Nottm to Annual Farriers' Dinner at the Welbeck. Returned on the last bus 11 pm.

Thursday February 13. Messiah performance at Clawson, Coys bus took 16 from Harby. Mr & Mrs H Furmidge, Mrs J Wilford, Mrs Dolman, Mrs C Buxton, Eva Mabbott, Mrs Bowles, Bab, Barbara, Martin & I, Ivy, Mrs Attewell & Ray Faulks & Mrs J Moulds. Good performance, 60 voices, 9 instruments

Sunday October 5. Sad news of loss of airship R101. Death toll 47 out of 54 on board.

On the last page of this volume above the date September 1930 is written out by Martin a poem by Douglas Malloch, "The Worker's Prayer". The last verse reads-

"God give me this, a chance to serve
Since I am served so well.
To draw the line, to shape the curve
To make my goods to sell.
But something that will help mankind,
With pleasure dreamed, with love designed,
Something that men can use & see
By which they will remember me."

Harby life

BUILDING Leslie Cram

Dan Coy built the bungalow in what was then called Steppings Lane before he and Babs Barlow were married in December 1929. He bought the plot of land in the corner of her paddock from Mrs Kemp for £20. The bungalow was bought as a kit consisting of a plan and all the necessary materials. The frame, floors and bottom half of the external wall cladding were timber and the upper walls, internal walls and ceilings were asbestos cement sheeting. The roof slates were also made of asbestos cement. It was built on a brick base with a brick chimney. There was a range of wooden buildings at the back consisting of a washhouse, coal shed and toilet with a two-hole pan closet, all connected to the house by a conservatory. His friend Ernie Dewey, John Dewey's father, built a similar one at Hose at about the same time.

In 1936 he dug a well to supply drinking water for the bungalow. It was about twelve to fourteen feet deep, lined with bricks, and Dan constructed a lead pump to bring the water to the surface. Before they had the well in their own backyard they had to fetch drinking water from a well in Watsons Lane. To get water for washing etc. Dan built a large brick cistern under the yard to collect the rainwater from the roof. This was pumped with a semi-rotary hand pump to a cistern in the roof from where it fed the hot and cold taps in the house. There was no bathroom but a full sized bath with hot and cold water supply was concealed under a large trap door in the kitchen floor.

About the same time as Dan Coy was building his own house in Steppings Lane, the council were building the row of council houses along the north side of School Lane. There was trouble with the water supply there as well. Avis Wright and her husband Ted were the first occupants of number 4. Avis remembers –

Stepping Lane, now called the Red Causeway, in 1929, The Box Bush, the house built by Daniel Coy when he got married in 1929. To the right and behind the house is Mrs Kemps Paddock. "Spot" the terrier dog is sitting in the porch. TCOY.

Harby: Village life in the Vale of Belvoir

"We had outside flush toilets, bathrooms and taps over the sink, but no water supply! We had a huge tank on top of the washhouse, connected to a tap in the kitchen, supposedly to catch rainwater for washing purposes - but unfortunately the tiles were porous, so it was some months before we caught any water. A pump was installed in No. 7's garden, but was found unfit for anything except toilet flushing, so we had to rely on good neighbours, who allowed us to fetch water from their garden pumps. My husband fetched two bucketsful each morning from Coy's garage, situated at the bottom of School Lane. That was to cook with, clean and wash. At one time, in the summer of 1937, I heated up a panful, to bath the baby, reheated it to wash nappies etc., reheated it again to wash the kitchen floor. We often borrowed a tub on wheels to carry water from the canal for washday - it was cleaner than it is now, but still had a peculiar smell and strange floating objects!"

THE CANAL

THE GRANTHAM CANAL : HISTORY AND FUTURE RESTORATION

Hugh Marrows, from "The romantic canal, alongside the Grantham pages 12 – 13 and 27.

A BRIEF HISTORY

Not surprisingly the good citizens of Grantham, well aware of the developing importance of Nottingham as a centre of what was then the latest in transport communications, were keen to have their own link into this expanding, and they hoped lucrative, system. Turnpike roads were still poorly surfaced and journeys remained difficult both for travellers and the conveyance of goods and produce. Furthermore, along with the rise in manufacturing industries and their associated urban developments, agricultural practices and productivity were improving just as these new town markets appeared. In Grantham too, businessmen would no doubt have known that within their home county the Louth canal linking that market town to the Humber at Tetney had opened in 1770 and that the Sleaford Navigation to the River Witham was under construction. It opened in 1794.

The route that eventually met with success began at Trent Lock in Nottingham and a Bill obtained Parliamentary approval on April 8th 1793, went through the Lords on the 17th and received royal assent on the 30th (incidentally 1793 was a canal boom year with nineteen new canals being authorised!). The euphoria at their success even encouraged the promoters to have a special song composed, expressing their enthusiasm in extravagant terms; a typical verse ran -

"The goddess shall her blessings unfold
Then open your treasures and pay down your gold
Our trade it will flourish - then freemen be bold
To finish our new navigation
To finish the Grantham Canal."

Harby life

A committee was set up under the chairmanship of Lord Brownlow of Belton House and £75,000 in shares was raised from businessmen in both Grantham and Nottingham. Construction began the same year. In overall charge of the work was William Jessop, a famous canal engineer, but two other principal engineers, James Green and William King, were also involved. Green was answerable to Lord Middleton of Wollaton Hall, Nottingham and was to supervise the construction of the canal from the Trent through Nottinghamshire to the Leicestershire border. King was agent to the Duke of Rutland at Belvoir, and was to look after the remainder of the route through Leicestershire and Lincolnshire into Grantham.

To limit costs the surveyed route took advantage of the topography of the Vale of Belvoir and as far as possible followed the contours of the southern slopes. The effect of this decision can be seen by making an 'as the crow flies' measurement from modern O.S. maps. This shows the distance from Trent Lock to Old Wharf, Grantham to be about 20 miles; by road (even today with modern by-passes) it is around 22 miles, yet the canal takes 33.

The rise of the canal has been variously quoted but the generally accepted figure is 139 feet 9 inches. The central pound produced by the circuitous route runs without locks for 20 miles. Even so 18 locks measuring 75' x 14' were still needed, plus over 60 bridges, numerous aqueducts and a few embankments and cuttings. These economies were also extended to other structures, brick bridges having been costed at about £120 and locks at £950 (including materials), but in spite of all this more money was soon needed and a further Parliamentary Bill in 1795 authorised another £30,000 investment. By February 1797, King's section was complete. Green was having trouble however near Cropwell Butler where puddling the canal bed with clay had been found necessary due to loss of water through the porous gypsum beds which lie close to the surface. Nevertheless the canal opened throughout by mid 1797, fulfilling the prophecy of a song published in the Stamford Mercury on 17th May 1793. There were seven verses, all in similar vein to verse three -

And thanks to heaven 'tis performed,
The poor will now be clothed and warmed
'Gainst wintry winds and tempest armed
Snug in their habitation
The young and old with equal joy
Will raise their voices to the sky
And children yet unborn will cry
"Blessed Grantham Navigation".

These lines contain a veiled allusion to the cost of coal in Grantham, hitherto exorbitant, which was expected to, and did, fall dramatically. The main cargoes 'in' were coal, lime, building materials and night soil from Nottingham for use as fertilisers, and various raw materials which allowed some manufacturing to begin in Grantham. Cargoes 'out' were primarily agricultural produce. The transit time was 2 days. It took a few years for the canal to become profitable, and there were problems along the way. In 1798 leakage through the gypsum beds needed attention, and this occurred again in 1804. By 1801 it was realised that the mile long Harlaxton Cut, which had been made too narrow to allow boats to pass each other, had become a genuine handicap and so passing places were cut.

In general however the canal lived up to its expectations and was returning a profit by the 1820s. Profits further increased until 1839, remaining steady until 1851 when the first railway reached Grantham. The town received additional benefits from the growth of manufacturing industries and also became a trading centre for corn and coal. The farsightedness of the Grantham Canal's promoters, and achieving their aim by 1797, is well illustrated when we remember that it preceded by several years other major canals such as the Kennet and Avon (1810) or the Leeds and Liverpool (1816).

The Ambergate, Nottingham, Boston and Eastern Junction Railway took over the canal in 1854 but within a few years this company had leased its entire operation to the Great Northern Railway. The GNR however, had little concern for the canal, seeing it as direct competition, and a slow decline began, accelerated by the railway's 'take over' of the iron ore trade from Woolsthorpe in the 1880s.

Inevitably the advent of the railway system during the mid 19th century had an impact upon the Grantham Canal - as it did on most others. But in some respects the Grantham Canal managed better than many, and it was not until the age of the petrol engine that closure came. Profitability, though declining, was sustained for some time, in fact into the 20th century. Respite came during the First World War when a military camp was opened in Alma Park, north of Grantham, and the canal was used to transport supplies. Trade declined rapidly after the war ended and ceased in 1929.

Marion Potter on the Swing Bridge over the canal at the north east corner of the Wong about 1953. The steel support bars from the two uprights on the right of the bridge helped to hold the opposite end horizontal. The bridge swung on a pivot below the uprights. It spanned the canal at all times until it was swung to allow a barge through, then repositioned to cross the canal again. NCUN.

Harby life

RESTORATION

Trade had declined to such an extent on the canal by 1929, and so much maintenance was required, that its owners, the London and North Eastern Railway (who had taken over from the GNR in 1924) closed down all commercial operations. Legal closure took longer and did not take full effect until 1936. The canal then lay unused (in the commercial sense) for over thirty years - or nearly so!

The canal served as an important land drain for local farmers, which largely ensured that the canal remained in water. This meant that by the 1960s, when there was a developing public appreciation of our industrial archaeological heritage and the stirrings of active consideration for its preservation, the Grantham Canal was by no means as derelict as it otherwise might have been. By the end of the 20th century therefore, with ownership having passed to British Waterways, the transition from a defunct commercial artery into the leisure amenity which we enjoy today, was well under way.

In 1969 the Grantham Canal Restoration Society (GCRS) came into being, and since then various other bodies such as the Grantham Navigation Association have also been formed. Today these, together with the Inland Waterways Association and local and county councils along its length, work together as the Grantham Canal Partnership.

The ultimate aim is to reopen the canal to navigation from the Trent to Grantham.

Swimming in the canal at the bottom of the Wong, perhaps around 1930. Left to right R Comb, Mac Hoyes, L Moulds. BTOW.

TOM WATCHORN OF HICKLING IN THE BELVOIR COUNTRY
by "Idler", from Harby News issue 4, pages 6 - 8.

The subject of this sketch could not claim to be anything but an ordinary man, but he was a true countryman who always had to battle with fearsome physical odds, and lived a life of usefulness in the Vale of Belvoir, and for most of it on the Grantham Canal which served the numerous villages throughout the thirty-three miles of its meanderings. The old waterway, constructed about 1793, passed through lovely country and some of the finest dairy pastures in England. Its early usefulness was to convey crops and other products wanted in the large towns, and to bring back coals, iron, timber, bricks and manufactured goods wanted on the land, and these dictates were, no doubt, influenced by the requirements of Belvoir Castle, residence of the Dukes of Rutland. There was a light railway (which can still be traced) for the purpose from Bottesford wharf.

Alas this abandonment is followed by closure and silting up of the canal itself, about which much is now appearing in the Press with prevention suggestions, but with little hope we fear. The maintenance costs would be appalling, for whatever use might be made of the canal, who could, and would, bear the expenditure?

Anglers are perhaps making the greatest outcry about canals being closed, and it was for fishing that Tom Watchorn was best known, and almost universally known to thousands of anglers all over the country. Born just over the Nottinghamshire border from Harby, in very early life he suffered from a paralysed leg, getting about on crutches, which gave him the not inappropriate soubriquet "Crutchy" by which he was always known, and perhaps more particularly to the children of the villages. He was remarkably active with the disability, and could do almost anything that others more favoured physically could do. He had some early apprenticeship to tailoring, which served him well in his modest and often poor circumstances. The latter did appeal to a band of anglers who visited Hickling often, and they subscribed to buy Tom a boat off the Trent, which served him so well for very many years, and almost to the end of his life.

Before we forget, let us record that this latter happening showed up the true character of the man, for in declining years, and with very limited means, he willingly chose the "big house" at Bingham, where he passed out comfortably and uncomplainingly well on towards the allotted span. He would not have had it otherwise. I had spent many a week's holiday with him, fishing from the boat, visiting a dozen villages over twenty miles and more off the old cut. With a box of groceries, etc. sent by carrier from Nottingham, we would set sail from Hickling Basin on Saturday morning for the week, living the truly primitive life, and knew no time or trouble.

The craft with marvellous ingenuity possessed everything, lockers fore and aft, seats boxed in solid, and other contrivances revealed bedding, complete changes of clothing and boots for Sunday best, tools for woodworking, boot repairing, tailoring, and other requirements. You could have haircut and shaving, teeth drawn, and balm for all ills prepared from nature's wayside products.

Harby life

Tom was medico for all sorts of people and things in the villages where he called; he would mend cycles, china, watches and clocks, write letters, and in fact was never at a loss for making a little money which was sorely needed. At holiday times he toured the boat hire, for which he was well known to parents and children with their pence.

He led a clean and good life, and with his natural disability and limited resources, could overcome almost any difficulty. He was never away from those villages, except for one day a year, when he made pilgrimage to the Nottingham Goose Fair, and to see the only one relative he ever knew. He respected Sunday, bathed in the canal, shaved and put on his Sunday clothes, complete with gold guard, and he had a four-course dinner fit for a king, and in this I often shared.

In extreme cold and snow, he had a hut ashore in The Plough yard at Hickling, very snug, and with his poor legs curled in like a hedgehog was always safe, and slept soundly. It was a good life of contentment making the best of circumstances, with no rent or rates or cravings. Who can deny.

CHEESE MAKING

WATSONS DAIRY
Mary Evelyn from "The Cheese of the Country" in Health, October 1927 pages 170 to 178.

In 1927 a national magazine on health was interested in cheese production in Britain and was directed to Harby and the Watsons in charge of the United Dairies factory here. The magazine published this account. Cheese making at Harby continued and flourished in the following years, apart from being suspended during the Second World War. Robert Watson in time took over from his parents as manager.

We perpetually grumble at our cooks and run down English cookery. Nothing can beat our British products, why shouldn't they also be sung? Take Stilton cheese for example; who invented that? First I rang up my friend, Mr. Appleford, buyer of the provisions for the Civil Service Supply Association, and asked his advice.

He told me the Vale of Belvoir was the district where the best is made, and Mr. Widgery of the Wilts United Dairies arranged for me to go to Harby and stay with the manageress there for a night or so, that I might see a full day's work. There are Cheddar and Cheshire and Dunlop and many other good local cheeses in England and Scotland, but Stilton is exclusively British.

CHEESE HISTORY.
Harby was chosen, not because it belongs to the United Dairies Limited, but because Mrs. Herbert Watson, the manageress has won the Silver Cup, three years running, at the Leicester Show and now is the Champion Stilton Cheese-maker of Leicestershire, and the owner of the Cup. It is said that real Stilton cheese can only be made in that part of Leicestershire of which Melton Mowbray is the centre and that the grass lands are so rich because they have never been touched by the plough.

Mrs. Watson is young and charming with lovely colouring, and full of enthusiasm and vitality. Her husband, who manages the place, is equally capable and interesting ; an extremely well-read man. The Stilton Cheese making at Harby is carried on on factory lines, although as may be seen from the photographs it looks like a farm dairy. The milk is, however, supplied by the neighbouring farms and comes in twice a day, morning and evening. Some send it; from others it is collected. There are four rooms, two up and two down; and the cellars; with a large open entrance place where the pans, cloths, etc., are washed and sterilised. Everything is scrupulously clean, and the temperature and ventilation are scientifically correct.

A Stilton cheese measures from 8 to 12 inches in height and some 8 inches across, and may weigh from 10 to 18 lbs. In appearance it is drab in colour, showing a curiously wrinkled rind like the net work markings on some varieties of melon. The rind should 'give,' but at the same time feel elastic under pressure from the fingers. When it is cut, it is a pale, creamy white, opaque, and interspersed with veins of 'mould' green, rather than blue in colour, at least in the earlier stages of ripeness. Of smooth velvet-like body, the texture gradually becomes open and in the end markedly flaky, though the firm silk-like consistency of the separate portions should be maintained. In the best textured cheese the mould radiates from the centre.

Mary Jane Starbuck Stilton cheese maker and devoted church worker, about 1900. She lived from 1858 - 1944, did not marry, and made and sold crab apple jelly to fund the original cocoa matting which covered the church floor until the late 1970s. CBOO.

Many makers sell the cheese at a month or six weeks old for the cheese merchants to mature in their own cellars. A cheese of this type seldom matures under four months and more often requires six before it is fit for the connoisseur's table.

At one time a Stilton cheese was not considered ripe for cutting until it was two years old, but this was by the old methods. With improvement in equipment, and more scientific knowledge, the ripening process is now shortened, and the best cheese is better than ever. This is the opinion of a connoisseur who is not financially interested.

CHEESE-MAKER'S LIFE.
The work of making is most arduous and fell heavily on the farmer's wife. Worked as a business Mrs. Watson considers it a most interesting occupation, but it is not everyone who will take the trouble to be interested. Those girls who do, enjoy it thoroughly. It requires hard work, much care and good judgment, but although the

judgment must always have been as good, the work must have been even harder in days gone by than it is to-day, because improved methods and appliances and up-to-date conditions make it easier.

To turn the cheese in the hoop is in itself an art, and requires much skill as may be imagined when one realises that each hoop contains about 26 lbs. of curd and salt.

Cheesemakers have to be up early in the morning. At Harby work in the dairy begins at 6.00 a.m., breakfast is at 7.30 a.m., and dinner at 12.30 p.m. Then everyone goes off duty until 4.30 p.m., when they all come on again until 6.30 p.m., to attend to the morning's curd and to take in and rennet the evening's milk. At 6.30 p.m. all go off and then take it in turns to come back at 8.00 p.m. and ladle off the curd.

About 1,200 gallons of milk are collected at Harby, and 70 cheeses turned out daily. The 200 to 250 pigs kept to consume the whey get fat. They are then sold to wholesalers in Nottingham and eventually find their way to small smokers.

Harby Stiltons are noted. Although last year was a bad season they were as good as ever and sold as well.

The advantage of being part of a big organisation is that there is never any lack of capital to supply all up-to-date needs, and whilst the produce is made in the country the organisation in the centre of the business world sees to all sales and watches the market. The farmer may be a very good farmer, but he may not be a good business man. The union of farming and business should be beneficial. Only those who have had their hearts broken through working with insufficient capital can realise what a comfort it must be not to lose a chance through lack of money.

There are other advantages; combined forces can work a business more economically, by utilising all by-products, manufacturing for their own needs, etc. Efficient working may enable such an organisation to keep prices at a reasonable rate. On the other hand the desire for high dividends may tend unduly to raise prices to the consumer without giving the producer his share.

It is of course the business of any commercial organisation to carry on as efficiently and successfully as possible. It is equally the housewife's job to see that she is not overcharged and that the producer is properly paid. Her traditional occupations have been removed from the home to the factory, but she still retains her administrative powers in the home if she cares to use them, and the release from heavy manual labour leaves her with more time and strength for administration.

She may still be the "lady", the bread-giver. As the founder (in her own home) of modern organised industry it is her business now to study the economics of the questions of production and distribution of which the first stage is the land and the last her dining-room table.

Harby life

Robert Watson in the cheese store about 1960. JWAT.

The dairy in Watsons Lane, Victoria Manchester turning the new cheeses in the 1970s. JWAT.

The dairy in Watsons Lane in the 1950s. Left is Ethel Haywood and right Chris Staniforth weighing the curds. JWAT.

Harby: Village life in the Vale of Belvoir

Harby life

As consumer she has unrivalled power; if prices are too low in one respect and too high in another, it is her business to exercise her powers of control and re-adjust them. She can do this if she knows how.

She will need to study very widely and deeply and act judiciously. It is useless to play at Housewives' Associations. Knowledge must precede talk, otherwise the result is only "hot air". Courses of social and industrial history, applied economics, and practical dietetics are the present need. Housewives' Associations can profitably work with food producers, without eliminating or trying to eliminate the useful and necessary middleman. From being home manufacturers, they can proceed to help (collectively) to keep the economic balance, between the farmers and distributors, by their weight as purchasers. This is a function housewives have so far never consciously exercised in England; but they have exercised it most successfully in Australia and America, with benefit to all concerned, even to the large commercial organisations they controlled; and most certainly to the farmers, and growers of raw produce, as well as to their own household purses. Their slogan might well be : "To see life sanely and see it whole". Their aim to give the children bread and cheese instead of burnt porridge without endangering anyone's immortal soul.

The world has need of the statesman spirit, as a protection against the professional politician, and self-seeker; and with this spirit a social conscience. Apart from that: "It is to be noticed, and that with no small degree of satisfaction, by those interested in the progress of agriculture that wherever a factory is established the farming of the neighbourhood begins to advance, and to rise in the scale of effective working. This, after all, is what but little thought is necessary to shew would be a natural result. It is an almost a necessity of the factory system that the milk supplied to it by the farmers shall be of the best possible quality; other than this will not do for the results they aim at; other than this will not therefore be bought by them".

Watsons Lane Dairy 1927, six girls making cheese, at the front left to right Olive Brown, Connie Dickman, Phyllis Dickman. Health, 1927, volume 6, number 40 page 175.

Watsons Lane Dairy 1927, moving the cheeses from the storage and maturing cellars to be packed into wooden boxes for transport. From left to right - Mr Wills, John Stokes, Arthur Adams, Phyllis Dickman, Winifred Kirk, Betty Starbuck, Connie Dickman. Health, 1927, volume 6, number 40 page 177.

HARBY FARMERS' DAIRY *Trevor Coy*

Most of the dairy farmers in the village made cheese in their farm kitchens and some like 'The Croft' on Main Street and 'Starbuck House' had purpose built cheese rooms. They then got together in 1918 and formed a co-operative to be able to produce Stilton more efficiently.

The original shareholders were Herbert Fairbrother, Akerman Dewey, Samuel Swingler, Jesse Swingler, Padge Rawlinson, Jim Wilford, Harry Furmidge, Joe White, Jack Haywood, Bill Stroud, Chris Gale and John Lamin who were all milk producers. Mr Fairbrother was chairman of the management committee and also the manager for many years. A cheese maker was employed and the dairy although not as big as the Wilts. United Dairy was an important employer of local people, mostly women.

Ybele Gerard Veen 'The Dutchman' was the first cheese maker; he was followed by my grandfather, Daniel Coy, who had worked there for several years. I never knew my grandfather but I understand it was not wise to get on the wrong side of him. If any of the farmers delivered their milk to the dairy after 8:30am they were likely to be told to 'take it back home and have milk pudding for dinner'. After his death in 1932 his daughter, my aunt, Mary 'Ciss' Coy took over. There was never a proper cheese maker after Ciss and the trade declined until the dairy closed down prior to being taken over by Tithby Dairy and then Long Clawson Dairies.

The building had had a previous use, I think as a brewery and had some very well built, although height restricted brick barrel vaulted cellars which were ideal to keep the cheese at a more or less constant temperature but very awkward to work in when turning or moving the cheeses. These cellars were filled in when Long Clawson who had bought the premises in the 1960s refurbished them.

Harby life

I got involved with the dairy after I left school in 1948 as my father Dan Coy and I made all the tinware for them, as we did for the dairies at Colston Bassett and Hose, and also did most of the maintenance work. We made 80 gallon milk pans, siles (brass mesh sieves fitting at the top of the pans), leads and drainers, making up pans and fillers, ladles and hundreds of cheese hoops. In the post war years the sheet metal factories which had made munitions and aircraft parts started to produce stainless steel dairy equipment. This was more expensive than the tinplate but much longer lasting and by the middle of the 1960s the tinsmithing work had about died out. I remember two other tinsmiths in Harby, Thomas Dickman with whom my father had been an apprentice, and Tom Stokes, both of them semi-retired.

Some surplus Avro Lincoln bombers were sold by the government to Argentina after the war and they were refurbished and their crews were trained at Langar. The father of one of the pilots came over to England at the time and took a liking to Stilton cheese with the result that we got the job of making the equipment to fit up a small Stilton dairy at his farm. This was our one and only export order but I never knew if any Stilton was produced in Argentina.

The workshop of Box Bush bungalow in the Red Causeway about 1947. Trevor Coy is making one of the tin hoops used in Stilton cheese production that he supplied to the Harby Farmers' Dairy. A watercolour painting by Trevor Coy. TCOY.

DOCTORS AND NURSES,

HEALTH CARE IN HARBY *John Blundy*

Doctors

During the 1930s and 40s prior to the formation of the NHS, Harby was served by three Doctors. They were Dr Atkinson, with a surgery at his house in Waltham on the Wolds, Dr Cuddigan, with a surgery at his house in Long Clawson and Dr Roche with a surgery at his house in Colston Bassett. These three doctors continued to serve the village after the introduction of the NHS in 1948 with free health care. Health care before the NHS had to be paid for by the patient who in many cases would pay into a club like the 'Oddfellows' which would provide some financial assistance when the member was sick.

The doctors had set days for visits to the village, sometimes on horse back, but would also attend emergencies. Before the telephone became a must have in most households a request for the doctor to call was initiated by writing your name on a slate (in the case of Dr Cuddigan) attached to the rear wall of 'The Nag's Head'. Doctors Atkinson and Roche operated similar systems. A box near the slate was used by the doctors to leave medicine in for collection by patients. This system continued into the mid 1960s.

Nurses

Nurse Hollis lived and supported the work of the doctors in the village. When Nurse Hollis retired Nurse Pat O'Brien took over and when she retired nursing care was provided by a team working from Melton Hospital and responding to requests from the local surgeries. Some funding for nursing care came from collections taken at cricket matches for the Nursing Cup.

Harby Lodge in the snow about 1950, Pat O'Brien the nurse and Reveller the dog. JWAT.

Harby life

Maternity Care

Antenatal care was provided at the doctor's surgery if confinement was to be at home or at St Mary's Hospital in Melton where most births eventually took place. Postnatal care was provided at St Mary's Hospital and child development/health care was provided at a clinic in a room at the chapel in Long Clawson by Nurse M Swingler of Stathern. National dried milk and orange juice could be purchased at this clinic. Nurse Swingler also carried out home visits to give advice and care.

Dental Care

During the 1930s and 40s a dentist had a visiting surgery at the home of Miss Gregg once a fortnight.

POEMS FROM AN INVALID BED *Molly Whittaker*

Molly Whittaker was confined to her bed by a crippling disease in her later years. The Home Help service called regularly once a day to look after her. The family lived in a house on the north side of Stathern Road at the east end of the village. She could see across the road to the willow tree on the south side.

Molly Whittaker aged 21 in 1931 on Stathern Lane small holding. NCUN.

MELTON HOME HELP SERVICE - THE GOOD SAMARITANS

The Melton Mowbray Home Helps
Are the kindest ever seen
As they go round town and countryside
In their uniforms of green.

They come and do your weekly wash
And clean your house right through
They cheer you up when you are sad
And cook your meals for you.

They go to help the old folk
Who often live alone.
It's with these ladies' kindly help
That they can live at home.

And when the stork decides to come
To bring a sister or a brother
It's then the Home Help comes along
To take the place of mother.

And so Home Helps please carry on
With a job that needs some pluck
And from one whom you have helped so much
I say thank you and good luck.

THE OLD WILLOW TREE
By Molly Whittaker

The willow tree across the way,
I gaze at many times a day,
The slender branches spread around,
The trunk I know is not too sound.

In Spring I see the buds appear,
By Summer all the leaves are there,
With leaves so green it looks so gay,
Amongst them I see the children play.

In the morning there's the thrush who sings,
Much happiness to me he brings,
I feel sure he stops in the willow tree,
Especially to sing for me.

It's when I hear the high winds blow,
I see the branches swaying to and fro,
I think of the men in their ships at sea,
And how dangerous their work must be.

In the Autumn when the leaves fall down,
The branches soon are bare and brown,
I realize then that Winter's near,
With cold weather, snow and Christmas cheer.

To other folk, it's just a tree,
And yet it means so much to me,
To lie and watch the old, old willow,
Who entertains me from my pillow.

Harby life
FARMING

FARMS AT HARBY IN THE 1950s *John Blundy*

The map shows 20 farms within the parish of Harby during the 1950s. All would be producing milk and supplying it to the two local dairies (Wilts. United Dairy located off School Lane and Watsons Lane, Harby Farmers' Dairy on Langar Lane) and Colston Dairy. This milk would be used in the production of Stilton Cheese. Some farmers would also retail some milk locally.

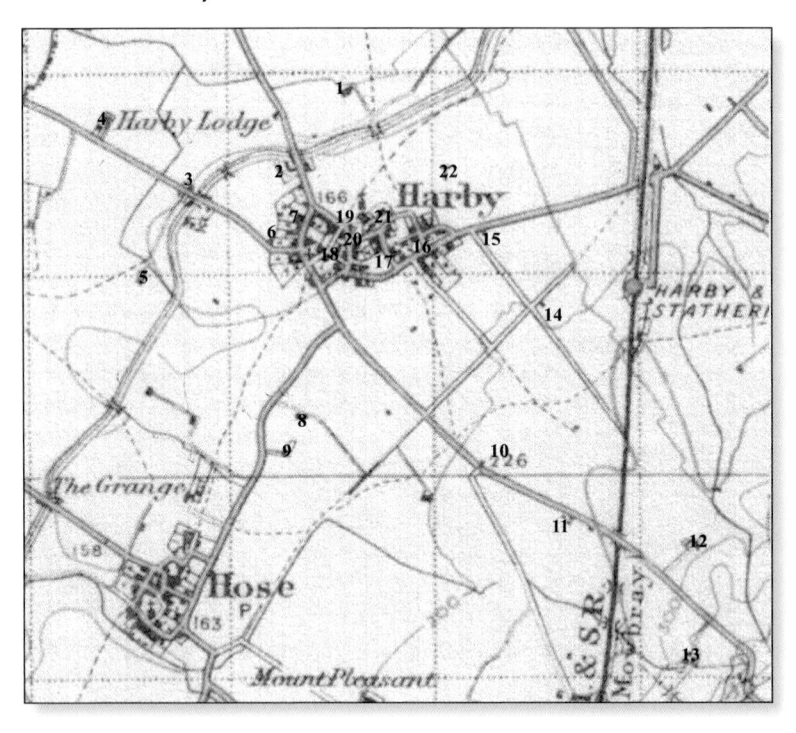

Number	1950 use	1975 and later use
1	Mr Kemp, working farm	Christian Mission Centre
2	Mr Wilford, working farm	residential use
3	Mr Lamin, working farm	working farm
4	Miss Rawlinson, working farm	residential use
5	Mr Scarborough, working farm	residential use
6	Mr Shipman, working farm	working farm
7	Mr Muxlow, working farm	working farm
8	Mr Barke, working farm	equestrian centre
9	Mr Mackley, working farm	poultry farm
10	Mr Nicholls, working poultry farm	poultry farm
11	Mr White, working farm	residential use
12	Mr Swingler, working farm	working farm
13	Mr Haywood, working farm	working farm
14	Mr Watchorn, working farm	disused
15	Mr Whittaker, working farm	storage
16	Mr Walker, working farm	working farm
17	Mr Dewey, working farm	residential use
18	Mr Pick, working farm	residential use
19	Mr Furmidge, working farm	residential use
20	Mr Tomlinson, working farm	residential use
21	Mr Pepper, working farm	residential use
22	Mr Coy junior, not built	working farm

Harby life

From the map it will be seen that very few of the farms now operate as such, the houses being used for private residences, barns converted into private residences and sheds and yards making way for new buildings. The land from these farms has been sold or rented out to other farmers. Willow farm in the 1950s was a poultry farm producing eggs, now it is an agricultural machinery sales and repair business. Mr Barke's farm is now involved in equestrian activities.

Only one new farm has opened in the parish since the 1950s, it has taken on land from some of the farms that have ceased farming, it is involved in milk production but this takes place in the parish of Stathern.

Les Whittaker with three of his breeding sows on Whittaker's farm on Stathern Lane about 1958. The feeding troughs are made from cut in half lorry tyres. DWHI.

Don Whittaker and a TE20 Ferguson tractor on the farm on Stathern Lane about 1949. The TE20 at an affordable price allowed tractors to lift loads as well as pull them along the ground and brought mechanisation to many farms. DWHI.

Harby: Village life in the Vale of Belvoir

Harby life

The reasons for the decline in milk production in an area known for its good pasture land are:

- Reduction in farm labour force due to mechanisation on the land resulting in shortage of labour to cover a seven day operation twice daily.

- Increased costs in production due to new regulations in the design and equipping of milking parlours in relation to collection and storage of milk.

- The introduction of milk quotas.

- Later the opportunity to sell their milk quota to bigger producers.

- Increased cost of feeding without an increase in the price of milk.

- Foreign imports of milk by supermarkets.

- The opportunity to turn pasture into arable land and grow new crops such as oil seed rape.

- The opportunity to convert farm buildings into residential accommodation.

- In the case of Harby many farms did not have a younger generation available or in cases willing to continue with farming.

The Dairy room at Whittaker's farm on Stathern Lane in the 1950s. DWHI.

A HARBY FARMING FAMILY *Leslie Cram*

The census returns and trade directories tell of Rawlinsons in Harby in the 1800s. But let us take up the story of the Rawlinson farming family in Harby in the early 1900s. Ernest Rawlinson with his wife Emma was a tenant farmer living in the old farmhouse on the corner of School Lane and Watsons Lane. His uncle Charles and his wife Anne with daughters Enid and Vera (nicknamed Queen) owned and farmed Harby Lodge Farm along the Colston Road. In 1926 Ernest and his family, now with children Peggy and Joan, moved to rent White House Farm which adjoined Harby Lodge Farm. The two families with girls of about the same age managed the two farms as one. Vera stayed at Harby Lodge Farm after her parents died and her sister moved to the Poplars in Watsons Lane on her marriage to Walter Pick. Ernest's family bought and moved to Sherbrooke Farm in 1942. Peggy married Leslie Shipman in 1943 and they took on Stathern Lodge Farm down by the canal. After Ernest's death in 1953 they moved to take over Sherbrooke Farm, retiring in the early 1980s.

These were mixed farms with the growing of corn, and the power coming from horses in the early years and then tractors, and combine harvesters. Cattle produced milk for the Harby dairies with the daily commitment of milking morning and evening, and there were sheep, pigs and chickens.

Sherbrooke Farm, Massey Harris combine harvester about 1950 JWAT.

Les Shipman in June 1952 in the paddock at Sherbrooke Farm milking the last Roan Heifer. JWAT.

Harby life

Harvesting with three heavy horses at Harby Lodge Farm about 1925. JWAT.

SHEEP FARMING IN HARBY IN THE 1930s *Harry Kemp*

This is a transcription of a tape recording of Mr Kemp, born in 1884, interviewed by Stanley Ellis in Harby, Leicestershire, in 1956, held in the Survey of English Dialects, © University of Leeds, accessed at the British Library Sound Archive, reference C908/56. It is available to be listened to on the internet on http://sounds.bl.uk/View.aspx?item=021M-C0908X0056XX-0500V0.xml#. The transcription is by Leslie Cram and John Blundy with the generous help of Jonathan Robinson from the British Library. The transcription gives the traditional spelling of the words without any alteration for how that word sounded in dialect.

A Mr Kemp is recorded with the Christian name Harry on the 1891 census as born in 1884 in Stathern but living in Harby. In the 1901 census he is described as an agricultural labourer, living with his parents. In later life he apparently had the nickname Gent. There is a photograph of him in uniform at the time of the First World War. The War Memorial records Kemp H having served. The sheep were washed by Washdyke Farm in the parish of Stathern where the stream comes down between the bridge over the railway and the turning of the road to Stathern.

Gent Kemp in uniform about 1915. CBOO.

86 Harby: Village life in the Vale of Belvoir

. . . used to shear with hand at one time and I would as about lief shear with hand as machine as far as that goes, cause if you had some as were turning they used to, you know, when they got [inaudible] would be like grinding an organ, instead of keeping going nicely. And them machines, they wanted them to go well else they're hard work and sweat well. And then they don't wash them now, you know. Get all the bits of stick and grit in, you soon do some blades in. It [inaudible] to the sheep, but you clip a horse what ain't been groomed much, it takes some getting through, don't it? They got it done first time.

Question: And they'd wash the sheep, would they?

Used to wash them across this pit here. Ah, about now they'd be busy washing, May, beginning of May and if we'd had any on them on turnips, well used to wash them twice. Wash them one week then again about nine or ten days after. 'Cause you know they get all sand and soil and such-like in them. And now they don't wash them at all.

Question: And how long would that take for one sheep?

Wash it? Oh not long, you'd perhaps bring a hundred down, there'd be about three or four on you, one chap in a tub, and two, two throwing in, perhaps two poling them, do you see, you'd pole them round, they had about five in the pit at once then he'd catch the one that'd been in the longest and turn it up and he'd have a spout, plenty of water stuck back, brought a stream up like that, do you see, and pull the wool about to swill them, do you see, then come out, come out of a narrow pathway and into a draining pen, stop there till you'd done the lot, and then if there were no more there, well they'd let them stand and come here up the pub then and have a pint or two of beer, do you see, and take off, of course if there were some more waiting well you hadn't much time, you'd got to have one quick and get off so as the others could get there. Oh ah, it used to be regular busy at that time sheep washing down here.

Question: Is that what that sluice is for?

That's it, that's it, you screw that down then to stop water to go all the back of that bank, do you see, then he'd have a wood plug in the hole of the sluice, pull it out and shove a long spout up to, wood spout and then there were a hole on the top, do you see, it come up here through the top of the spout, not direct straight, then it made it rise up like a spout, you know and drop a bit more force on them. And he'd turn them over and swill them all underneath and keep pulling the wool about to swill them. Oh ah, it used to be a rum job.

Question: Would that sort of make the fleece more valuable?

Oh yes, yes, it were worth more, but it didn't weigh so much when you'd washed it you know, you lose it in the weight. Then they got years ago so as they said, you needn't bother washing them, you can get it out when they get them clipped, but of course it weighs heavier but you don't get so much price per pound as you used to do. Well, what, do you know what I mean, you get more now cause it's a better price, wool is, but if it'd been them times unwashed wool wouldn't come nowhere near so much as washed wool, do you see. And they clip so much nicer then.

Question: Did you clip them up on, uhm, a wooden … ?

No, on the ground – sit them up, start, do left side first you should do, and then meet it with your right hand, but some'll start the right hand then start the back and go round. It's easiest then – one, like, side looks short and where they make, going the same road as the wool it's about that length then. Oh, I know, I've heard of folks having them on a pig cratch to clip them. I used to set them on the ground, it's a back-aching job, but it's all right when you get into it.

Question: And how many would you do in a day?

Well it depends, you see, we'd milking to do night and morning. We used to do about forty, you know, a day practically or rough speaking, might do odd more or might do a few less, would just depend. You'd got to milk, then fetch them up. Course my dad, when he were a lad, when I were a lad he always used to clip with shears and clip a lot. It used to be about two and nine-pence a score them days, three bob were a good price. Now they get about two pound a score I think. Ah, clipped plenty at two and nine-pence a score. We used to reckon two, two score then with shears.

Question:. Of course the money's not worth any more is it, even when they get two pound?

No, no, surprising what it is …

Vera Rawlinson with the dog at a picnic at harvest time at Harby Lodge Farm about 1925. The crop has been cut and put into stooks to dry before the grain is removed. JWAT.

THE GLEANERS *Betty Holyland*

The rough and stubbled fields glow bronze,
As sunshine heralds in the day,
Amidst the pyramids of corn,
Gleaners are gathering what they may.

Women and children wind their path,
Stooping for strands of wheaten gold,
Binding their finds with wisps of straw,
Ready for taking home to fold.

The day is hot and tired arms
Tend to the babes who quietly lay,
Shaded inside a nest of sheaves,
Out of the noon time heat of day.

Autumn tints on the hedgerow near,
Charm the scene to a passer by,
As softly wafts the gleaners' song,
Against the sweet and scented sky.

Behind the big thatched rick they rest,
And in its shade spread out their share,
Of food prepared before daylight,
With much concern and loving care.

Their Holland bonnets cast aside
They drink sweet elder beer and tea.
Closing their eyes in quiet peace,
Content in kindred company.

But not for long the blackbird shrills
Its warning cry against the clocks.
The gleaners carry on their task,
As lengthening shadows gild the shocks.

The evening light is failing fast
And far away a night-jar calls,
The gleaners wend their weary way
Eager for home 'ere darkness falls.

From its hiding place a stoat appears,
Running along the stubbled field.
Scenting the food from mid-day fare,
Discarded from the gleaners' meal.

Halting his run he has his fill,
Then disappearing with the day.
Blending with shadows on the hill,
He too a gleaner in his way.

Harby life

AUGUST Betty Holyland

Roses in the hedgerow,
Birds upon the nest.
Spellbound summertime,
The season I love best.

Poppies nestling in the corn,
To hide their crimson faces,
Belvoir lanes are full and deep,
With fairy flowers and graces.

IRONSTONE MINING

IRONSTONE MINING AND THE INCLINE

D L Franks from "Great Northern and London and North Western Joint Railway" pages 26 - 7.

South of Harby and Stathern Station and just south of the public road from Harby to Eastwell was the Stathern Ironstone Siding. The signal box was on the down side and directly opposite were the sidings and loading drop. The sidings consisted of two lines on either side of the drop, so arranged that the empty wagons coming from the north were shunted into the north sidings, from whence they ran by gravity to the drop and, when loaded, continued by gravity to the sidings on the south side. With this fall the sidings were steeply graded and caused some difficulty for engines to draw out the loaded trains. The rope hauled incline was installed in 1880. The drop was fed by a narrow gauge railway which came down the hillside by a rope-worked incline. At the top of the hill the narrow gauge railway served many mines in the district around Eastwell and Eaton, and extended up to the Great Northern line to Eaton. As many as three trains left the Stathern sidings daily in the best days, with destinations such as Stanton, Staveley, Renishaw and Parkgate. Some of the ironworks owned mines themselves, but most of the mining was done by small individual firms. These sidings were the last working point on the Joint Line, with the exception of the Redmile petrol depot.

Looking north over the parish of Harby from Harby Hills on 21 April 1960. The village is on the skyline. In the foreground is the incline taking iron ore to the main railway line. Full wagons go down on the left, empties come up on the right. SLEL.

Harby life

At the bottom of the ironstone workings incline about 1925. Full wagons came down on the track on the right, empties went back on the left. BTOW.

On the incline which took the ironstone down the hill to the railway, looking south up to the top of Harby Hill. Ernie Towers worked at the base of the incline transferring the ironstone into mainline wagons and here he stands about 1955. BTOW.

Hurst's Face ironstone quarry, Eaton about 1910. One of the workmen is probably Dora Butcher's father William Alfred Mabbott. The ironstone is loosened from the face by pickaxes and put into the wagons using the large forks. Another team clears the overburden above the working face, collecting small ironstone pieces in wheelbarrows and tipping these into the wagons from the raised boards over the tramway. DBUT.

Harby: Village life in the Vale of Belvoir

Harby life
LACE MAKING

LACE MAKING IN HARBY Leslie Cram

The Lord of the Manor for Harby and many villages around was the Duke of Rutland. He opposed having lace factories in his villages so Harby never had any factory, unlike Stathern under one of the Cambridge Colleges, where the factory building still stands and was operated by the Braithwaite family from 1841 until 1920.

In Harby arrangements were made with big factories in Nottingham for individual people to work on lace in their own homes. People in Harby today recall that relatives in the 19th century did this work and lace making is recorded in the census returns. The earliest return, for 1841, gives no details of employment status. In 1851 however there are 32 working as lacerunners, all young girls. In 1861 the figure is 8, 1871 has 3, 1881 only two and none in the following census returns.

A view from the roof of the Methodist chapel in the 1960s onto the White Hart with the window in the roof at the far end. This gave light to the Lace Room below where lace working was done. TCOY.

CHENILLE WORKING, A COTTAGE INDUSTRY IN THE VALE OF BELVOIR.
Jim Fisher

Chenille working for the lace trade was started in the Vale some time in the mid 1700s. Chenille making consists of putting spots on netting for ladies' wear and the work was done by hand on wooden frames. Chenille, a fine wire covered with a kind of silk, is twisted through the netting to form a spot and then clipped. The netting and chenille were provided by Nottingham firms for whom the "spotting" was done as outwork and then returned to the warehouse. Ever since lace itself became an industry, Nottingham has had the reputation of being its home, but few have realised the valuable assistance given by ladies from this part of the Vale of Belvoir to maintain that reputation. With the advent of the railway coming to this part of the Vale in the late 1800s the cottage industry boomed, with the labourers' wages so low it was the primary means of supplementing the family income in Harby, Hose and Long Clawson. An experienced chenille worker could easily place up to 1,000 spots an hour on lace. About 1910 the payment was 2 ½ d per 1,000 spots, but an extra few shillings a week was a godsend to the family income.

A Mrs Ann Clayton (1866 – 1945) was the business woman behind the boom. Her family had been chenille working for over 100 years in Long Clawson. With the railways coming it was much easier to have the goods delivered and returned from the local railway station. She was the main agent of thirteen lace warehouses in Nottingham and had over forty local ladies doing the chenille working at home. And the work could not have been done without their dedication.

One of the most treasured possessions of her family is a letter from Queen Mary thanking her for the making of a wedding veil of white chenilled net for the Princess of Teck on her wedding, saying how interesting it was to know that such work was done by ladies in the Vale of Belvoir.

Her daughter, Mrs G Hourd, carried on the business when it restarted after the Second World War, but it petered out in the 1950s when new mechanical machinery methods were introduced.

PARISH COUNCIL

THE PARISH COUNCIL *Anne Dames*

In the 1800s and early 1900s Harby had its own parish council. On the 29 January 1931 a joint Parish Council was formed. This combined the three Parish Councils of the villages of Long Clawson, Hose and Harby. Since then the joint Parish Council has consisted of eight elected representatives, three from each of the villages of Long Clawson and Harby and two representing the village of Hose. The election of Parish Councillors takes place every four years.

Matthew Towers about 1950 halting in his job as council street sweeper for Harby. Matthew was also church warden. BTOW.

POLICING

THE VILLAGE POLICEMAN AT HARBY *John Blundy, son of Harry Blundy.*

Until the late 1960s the village had its own policeman living in the village and working a beat including the parishes of Harby, Stathern, Eaton and Eastwell. Up to the early 1950s the beat was covered on pedal cycle, then autocycles were introduced, these were powered by a 50cc two stroke engine. In about 1954 the James 125cc motor cycle became the beat transport. About 1954 the Section Sergeant was provided with a Morris Minor to cover his visits, prior to that date he used his own transport.

The Bottesford Section covered the north east section of the county up to the borders with Nottinghamshire and Lincolnshire and the parish boundaries of Waltham on the Wolds on the A607 road, Scalford on the Eastwell to Scalford road and Hose on the Harby to Hose lane.

Harby life

Special Sergeant William Coy and Policeman Harry Blundy outside the old house at the south end of School Lane by Watsons Lane about 1950. They are standing just as policemen are expected to stand. HCOY.

The beat strength consisted of a Sergeant and Police Constable at Bottesford, a Police Constable at Redmile, a Police Constable at Croxton Kerrial and a Police Constable at Harby.

A series of points of contact were part of a period of duty. These were usually Post Offices, pubs and other locations with telephones, during the war and, until its closure, the police lodge at A V Roe's (just inside Nottinghamshire) was a point. Other points some, without phone contact were Eaton Crossroads, Eastwell Crossroads and Stathern railway bridge. These were so that senior officers from Melton could visit and check that pocket books were up to date. The senior officers would also visit the police house, check and sign the diary that the policeman kept.

Before the telephone was installed in the police house, urgent telephone messages were sent to the home of William Coy (special sergeant) and then taken the 200 yards to the police house. The police gazette came by post and provided details of local and national crime with pictures of most wanted criminals; these were all filed and stored for future reference.

The Chief Constable, a retired colonel, also paid an annual visit. He would inspect the house and garden, diary, pocket book, and equipment including police lamp, truncheon and handcuffs. During this inspection my father stood to attention in his uniform including white gloves. He was inspected and questioned on items in his diary and pocket book.

The work pattern was usually two shifts of 4 hours' duration planned by the Constable and approved by the Sergeant. The hours between 1 am and 6 am were rarely covered except for occasional patrols of Belvoir Woods to search for poachers. The daily routine would consist of patrolling the beat, making stops at contact points, making routine enquires regarding complaints received and observation of the movement of strangers in the district. On one occasion an escaped Borstal inmate was apprehended and locked in the outhouse until collected by staff from the Borstal at Lowdham.

The Village Policeman was responsible for:-

- Checking firearm certificates.

- Checking gun licences.

- Checking Dog Licence exemptions. Farmers with working dogs could have exemptions for certain dogs.

- Supervision of sheep dipping; read Harry Kemp's account of this activity in this book.

- Issue of movement orders during outbreaks of swine fever. These were required for movement of pigs from one part of a farm to another.

- Supervision of burning of an animal that had died or been slaughtered as a result of anthrax or foot and mouth disease including digging the pit, obtaining the fuel and burial of the ashes.

- Obtaining premises for Weights and Measures Officers to carry out testing and checking of equipment used in the sale of goods.

- Holding local vehicle checks each quarter of the year, checking vehicle excise licences (called road fund licences in those days and only issued quarterly or yearly) and insurance certificates.

- Cleaning and heating the Court House at Belvoir. This was located adjacent to the Dowager Duchess's house near the entrance to the estate offices. The court was held on the first Monday in the month.

- Other duties included attendance at the Hunt Puppy Show at Belvoir Kennels. The hunt let local farmers have the fox hound puppies for exercise and on their return to the hunt they were paraded and judged.

- Undertaking full night duties at the Hunt Ball at Belvoir Castle and various social events at hunting lodges in Melton.

The district was fairly free of major crime but in 1947 thieves broke into Harby and Stathern railway station and burnt down the booking hall and waiting room. They were

Harby life

caught in Nottinghamshire and stood trial. In the early 1950s a group of professional card players attended local whist drives which were qualifying heats for a final at Belvoir Castle, the first prize being a refrigerator or washing machine. The local Sergeant and PC observed these activities and at a later stage the CID arrested and obtained convictions for card sharping offences. In the autumn of 1957 the local policeman was called with a local doctor to attend a domestic incident at a keeper's cottage in Stathern woods. The injured person died from the injuries sustained in the attack, the attacker was arrested, convicted of murder and sentenced to life imprisonment. The Police House was closed and the house sold in 1967; this change was due to police policy of using Panda cars based in Melton.

Below is a list of officers who served at Harby.

- The trade directories of 1846 show a Thomas Garton as Police Officer at Harby. In 1858 he was at Market Bosworth
- PC W Blackwell 1914 to 1925
- No Policeman appears to be stationed at Harby for the next 18 months. This may have been due to a change of house as His Grace The Duke of Rutland sold property and the police house as I know it came into ownership of the Coy family.
- PC A White 1927 to 1929
- PC S J Hacket 1929 to 1934
- PC H Blundy 1934 to 1957
- PC R Fortnum 1956 to 1961
- PC P Atkins 1961 to 1962
- PC P Handley 1962 to 1967
- Special Sergeant W Coy served at Harby for many years and in the 1950s and 60s was supported by Special Constable T Sadler and Special Constable J Holdsworth

THE RAILWAY

HARBY AND STATHERN STATION

D L Franks from "Great Northern and London and North Western Joint Railway" pages 25 - 6.

Just over three miles from Redmile was Stathern Junction, sited in bleak fields, without habitation within view. It was a straightforward simple junction, no sidings, but equipped with a cross-over. A branch came trailing in from the west from Saxondale Junction on the Great Northern Nottingham-Grantham line, a little over seven miles away.

Sixty-two chains south of Stathern Junction Harby and Stathern Station stood in open fields. The original plans provided for this station to be built near the public road from Harby to Stathern on the embankment which exists there. It was found that the cost of making up the ground was too much so the station was built in the awkward place at the mercy of all the elements. Nothing can be found as to why the station was built in the fields, but as it was the chief exchange station of the Joint Line and built on a larger scale than other country stations, assumption can only be made.

Harby and Stathern station on a postcard dated 1916. On the platform on the left the boy on the right nearest the track is Archibald Octavius Harwood on his way to school at Sedgebrook. NCUN.

Harby: Village life in the Vale of Belvoir

Harby life

Harby and Stathern was the exchange station for all traffic and a more unlikely one it is hard to visualise. It was a most awkward station to work, nearly everything was placed to be least handy. The first example of awkwardness was the turntable, it was at the northern end of a siding on the west side of the station and could only be reached by intricate moves through intervening sidings. Next the sidings were insufficient for the amount of traffic in the peak days and much congestion resulted. The passenger train accommodation was even more difficult from a working point of view. The platform faces consisted of the two through main lines, on the west side a through platform face existed, but the line serving it connected with the down main line, only to the up, by a trailing connection. Thus down trains could not enter directly. Visualise a normal working; a Great Northern train from Leicester would run to the down main line platform, perform station duties, move ahead and reverse to the "West" platform to await the London and North Western train from Market Harborough and take on any passengers there might be for the Grantham direction. After the departure of the LNW train the GNR train would leave for Grantham. This used to be more complicated when the Great Northern Newark-Northampton service ran. Then for a short period the Newark to Northampton trains terminated at Harby and Stathern, and these trains had to be disposed of in the sidings until the other passenger trains finished their work and left.

Next consider the working in the other direction. Again a Great Northern train would run to the up main line platform, perform station duties and then move ahead and back into the bay siding. Incidentally this was not truly a bay, but a carriage dock, but it had a face to the up platform. If the train had more than two six-wheel coaches and a small engine the bay could not hold them and the train would have to be shunted across to the "West" platform, thereby disrupting down line working. The station was very inconvenient for local passengers with the approach road some five hundred yards long.

The staff of Harby and Stathern station after the fire in 1946. From the left to the right the names are - Sam Gregg, Dorothy Pearson, George Beard, Reg Pritchett, Herbert (Tilly) Manchester, Nigel Reeves, George Haynes, Michael O'Leary, Joe Cunnington, Sam Hourd, Alf Richmond, Len Rimmington, Ken Chambers.
BTOW.

Harby life

The Harby platelayers gang about 1945, at Barnstone. From left to right they are Ken Furmidge from Stathern, Mick O'Leary from Harby, Ted Munro from Stathern, Joe Cunnington the Ganger from Harby, Cecil Moulds from Harby, Sam Widdowson from Barnstone. NCUN.

The last goods train that ran on the Melton to Colwick line before it closed, crossing the bridge on Stathern Lane on 7 February 1964. Watercolour painting by Vic Millington. VMIL.

The goods yard was very large. There still stands the original warehouse, which was well equipped with a wagon weigh on the shed line and a large office, divided into two, with accommodation for six to eight clerks. In the yard were a number of cabins used by the Signal and Telegraph Department, it being the headquarters for the Joint Line. The Engineers had their district inspector's office here, together with a store. The other cabins were used by shunters, goods porters and plate-layers gangs. Another cabin was used by the Railway Clearing House number-takers. There was also an oil store for the whole of the line.

The signal box was on the up platform at the southern end, containing 36 working levers and 16 spare. The "West" platform was controlled at both ends from the box and it was signalled in both directions. The south end of the goods yard was controlled by a ground frame, with release from the signal box. On the down platform was a very unusual name board. The uprights carrying the board were extended in height and had brackets for lamps, which performed the dual duty of illuminating the name board and lighting the platform.

Harby life
RETAILING

VILLAGE SHOPS.   *Peggy Shipman, edited by Leslie Cram*

In the early part of last century the blacksmith's forge stood at the lower end of School Lane, opposite the present garage. There were also three carpenters, one near Diamond Cottage - Nether Street, one on Green Lane - Rutland Villa and the Wheelwrights were the Martins. There were two bakers, the Martins (where now Claude Rawlings lives) and the Watchorns (where Miss Freda Lane lives). The Watchorns were also butchers. The other butcher's shop was at Jackson's Farm (Mr George Dewey's).

In Dickmans Lane, a general store and tinsmith's was kept by Mr Dickman at Ambleside. Dove Cottage was a Dame's School (100 years ago 2p per week was paid for a little child of 3 years). A general small shop was kept at the north end of Green Lane opposite Walker's Farm. There was a cycle shop where Gas Walk joins Boyers Orchard which also had a petrol pump. Lilac Cottage sold cakes. By the War Memorial was Bradwell's shop in the 1960s which had previously been run by the Whyles and the Hollands. Exchange Row had its shop which was first of all run by the Browns, later Harrimans. Finally there was the Post Office and shop on the corner of Dickmans Lane and Boyers Orchard.

Harby Post Office around 1900 in Watsons Lane. The sign sticking out from the wall reads "HARBY POST OFFICE". Below this the sign announces the services offered "Post Office for money order, savings bank, parcel post, telegraph, insurance and annuity business." In the doorway is Mrs Kemp who kept the Post Office then. The post box is set in the bottom right of the window. The village bakery was in the building behind the Post Office. BTOW.

Harby life

HOME SHOPPING AT HARBY 1940s TO 1960s   *John Blundy*

Long before Iceland and Tesco started home deliveries, firms had taken orders and delivered goods into homes in the village. W Coy had a carriers business in the 1920s and brought goods back to the village.

Melton Mowbray Co-operative Society had a representative call and collect order books for groceries early in the week and they were delivered later that week. In the 1950s they changed the system and had a travelling shop about the size of the library van of today, it had a door at the rear for customer access and goods on shelves on either side. The assistants would either collect your order book, make up the order and bring it to the house, or you could go on the van and select your own goods.

Brown's shop in Nether street around 1895. From left to right the people are, behind the cart an unidentified lady, Arthur Brown (born 1880) in the cart, John Brown (born 1837) at head of the horse, Lizzie (born 1881) and Rose Brown (born 1876) stand at the shop door, William Brown (born 1882) has the bicycle. JWRI

Several drapery and haberdashery shops from Melton including the Co-op, Brotherhoods, Manchesters and Doncasters from Bingham had representatives call weekly taking orders for ladies' and gents' clothes, household linen, floor covering and curtains etc. They would deliver the goods the following week or if they were large items they would be delivered by a van.

Melton Co-op delivered milk several times a week; this was in competition with Long Clawson Dairy. The Co-op Dairy closed in Melton as the supermarkets started selling milk. Long Clawson continued to deliver until Express Dairies took over. In the 1940s and 50s farmers also retailed milk.

Hardware, cleaning materials, pots and pans were available weekly from Mr Baines of Bingham, Sharpes Stores and Picks Stores of Melton. They had vans of about 30 cwt capacity with side openings to allow display and access to the goods. Mr Baines had a tap on the rear of the van connected to a paraffin storage tank in the van. Paraffin was used by some people for heating and for cooking stoves.

Harby life

Outside the slaughter house at the corner of School Lane and Nether Street where the garage now stands. Harry Starbuck left and Matt Towers with a sheep's carcass about 1940. BTOW

The Post Office in Burden Lane in 1927, from left to right Lizzie and Fred Pepper who ran the shop and Jack their son aged 9. CBOO.

The house which had previously been a shop on the corner of Stathern Lane and Green Lane about 1912. In the doorway is Alice Cunnington, on the left is Ada Cunnington, in the middle is Albert Cunnington and the girl on the right is Gladys Cunnington. NCUN.

102   Harby: Village life in the Vale of Belvoir

Harby life

Several bakers came into the village. They were Jessons from Hose, Whittakers and Allens from Long Clawson. They all baked their own bread. Jessons had Jowett-Bradford delivery vans and then Standard Atlas vans. Whittakers usually had Ford 10 cwt vans. Ernie Allen had a horse drawn cart which knew the round. The story goes that one night Ernie had gone to sleep in the cart and persons unknown turned the horse round and it went back towards Hose. A few years ago this bread cart was on display in the museum in Melton.

Harby had its own butcher and slaughtering facilities run by Akerman Dewey until the late 1950s at Jacksons farm. Arthur Miller and T Hall and Sons came from Stathern, Pells from Plungar and A E Pears from Long Clawson. In addition Watkins from Grantham used to come round weekly with cooked meats and pork products. Mobile fish and chip vans used to come into the village weekly. They were the Windsor Bar from Grantham, Harrisons from Melton and latterly Jim Fisher from Hose. Arthur Mawson operated a mobile greengrocery business from Harby serving Harby and surrounding villages. John Dewey took over this business when Arthur retired. Skinner and Rook Beer, Wine and Spirit Merchants of Nottingham had a representative visit your home, take the order and later that week the delivery was made.

The village had three shops as well as being served by these travelling traders.

The Cross and War Memorial about 1965 showing Horseshoe Cottage with Bradwell's shop on the right of the cross. The shop was run by Mabel Stead the blacksmith's wife into the 1940s, then Mr Whitehead took over from her. The Wyles family operated a fish and chip shop and a grocery store in it into the early 50s. After them the Holland family took over the shop and finally the Bradwell family. CBOO.

Harby life
WINDMILLS

HARBY WINDMILLS *Leslie Cram*

The 1777 and 1790 maps of the village show by an illustration of a post mill, where the sails turn to face the wind on a large post set in the ground, that the earliest Harby windmill stood on the high ground catching the prevailing south west wind on the south side of the road to Hose. The 1884 map shows this mill and two other tower mills, where the sails revolve to face the wind at the top of a brick tower, one at Langar bridge and one at Colston bridge. They both caught the wind and also were positioned by the canal to receive grain and then send it out after milling. The 1904 Ordnance Survey map shows only the Colston bridge mill remaining. The census returns and the trade directories give us excellent details going back to 1846 of the names of those employed at the mills.

The early photographs of the mills are all of the Colston bridge building. This tower mill was rated the finest in the county, and one of the finest in Britain. It was built in 1828 and stood seventy-three feet high to the top of the ball finial. In 1836 the nearby granary building which still stands was built alongside the canal. The mill ceased to make flour about 1916 due no doubt to government rules introduced at that date. However, it continued to grind pig and poultry food.

Harby mill at Colston Bridge about 1925 showing sails and the gallery. FBAN

By 1912 the granary building had been converted to take a steam engine and the miller is recorded in the trade directory as "Walter Stubbs, miller, steam and wind". In 1922 this had become an oil engine. In 1938 the fantail which had the function of directing the sails into the wind, was in poor condition and the blades broke allowing the mill to be tail-winded. The sails were wrecked. The owners did not repair the mill but sold what they could for scrap. Later, the building of the aerodrome at Langar led to the top floors being demolished, as the mill was now on the aerodrome approaches. This left the tower only four storeys high, and it is now a store.

Harby windmill about 1930. From left to right John Lamin, his son Edward, and his sister Dorothy with the milk cart. FBAN.

2. HARBY IN THE WARS

FIRST WORLD WAR

1920 WAR MEMORIAL STORY *Neil Cunnington*

Dating from the early 1920s we have an excellent photograph and an oil painting showing the front view of the War Memorial cross erected in honour of the Harby soldiers and sailors who participated in The Great War. A committee was formed in the village to get drawings, estimates etc. The accepted plans were drawn up by Mr T Burbidge, and the work was entrusted to Mr S Squires of Bingham. The total height is nearly fifteen feet, the lower of the two bases being eight feet square. The stone above is four feet square and two feet in height containing ninety-nine names, nineteen on the front face being those who made the great sacrifice. The remaining eighty names are those who also enlisted from the village and survived the ordeal of The Great War. Surmounting this stone is an old shaft and base from the ancient village cross, which was dismantled by Cromwell's Roundheads in their crusade against everything that did not conform to their puritanical beliefs. This is capped with a new cross from a suggested design of what the original may have looked like, and drawn by a former rector of the village, the Rev. Manners Octavius Norman. The whole of the structure, both old and new, is of Portland stone. It is particularly fitting that the old pillar should be used as this relic of the old village cross stood originally on the village green, not many yards from its present position. When the school was built in 1860 it was removed into the churchyard where it had stood until used as this Memorial. The unveiling ceremony took place on the night of Thursday, 20th May, 1920, and was performed by the Rev. E H Stone, Rector, in the presence of two hundred people. An impressive service was held before the dedication, in which the church and chapel choirs sang, and sixty ex-servicemen formed a guard of honour. The Rev. Stone, in the course of his address, expressed his gratitude to the ex-servicemen of the village for the part they had played in the winning of the war. The Rev. C T Lander, Wesleyan Minister, Long Clawson, said it would have been impossible to erect a more fitting Memorial. After the 1939-45 war, two names of men who did not return were carved on the base. The stones of the original cross extend two thirds of the way up the column. The upper third and the decorated cross at the top of the column is all new work. The together was made by Mr Martin Stead, the village blacksmith.

Oil painting by Guilford Wood of the War Memorial soon after it was erected in 1920. BTOW.

Harby life

The inscription at the front reads

ERECTED BY THE PARISHIONERS IN MEMORY OF THOSE WHO FOUGHT IN THE GREAT WAR 1914 1919

BAILEY J. T.	MABBOTT F.W.
COOK E.	MOULDS C. H.
DEWEY E.	MOULDS G. H. *D.C.M.*
GOODSON B.	RAWLINGS T.
GREAVES W. H.	SMITH J.
HALL H.	STOKES A.
HAND B.	WESSON F.
HOYES F.A. *M.M.*	WOODFORD L.
HOYES J.	WRIGHT W.
KEMP T.A.	

OFFERED UPON THE ALTAR OF THE NATION.

The three other sides contain the names of all who fought and lived.

BEND T.	GREGG S.	MUSSON F. J.
BILBY R. H.	HALL T.	MUSSON J. S.
BROWN A. R.	HAYWOOD A.	MUSSON W. J.
BROWN G.	HAYWOOD J.W. *BG. M.M.*	OXBROUGH T. H.
BROWN W.	HERRICK G.	OXBROUGH J. J.
BROWN W. H.	HOYES F. E.	OXBROUGH J.W.
BURBIDGE T.	KEMP E.	OXBROUGH W. S.
BUTCHER H.	KEMP C. C.	PEPPER F.
COOK E.	KEMP H.	PICKARD J. M.
COY A.	KNAPP W.	RAWLINSON R.
COY C. E.	KNIGHT A. J.	REEVES G.
COY D.	MABBOTT A. E.	ROSE G.W. *D.C.M.*
COY I.W.	MABBOTT H. E.	ROSE L.
COY J.T.	MABBOTT W.A.	ROSE S. J.
CROFT C.	MANCHESTER H.	SHIPMAN T.
DALBY C.	MARTIN E.	SHELTON T.
DEWEY C. E.	MEADOWS R. A.	SKINNER L.
DEWEY J.A. *BG. C. DE G.*	MILLER R.W. *M.C.*	SMITH A.
ELLIOTT D.	MOULDS A. E.	SMITH H.
FURMIDGE J. S.	MOULDS G. S.	SMITH T.
FURMIDGE T. H.	MOULDS H.W.	STARBUCK G.
GLOVER W.	MOULDS J. I.	STARBUCK S.
GRAY E. C. *D.C.M.*	MOULDS J.T.	STARBUCK W.T.
GRAY J.	MOULDS J.W.	STEVENS H. E.
GRAY W.	MOULDS S.	WALKER L.
GOODSON J.	MOULDS W.	WRIGHT J.
GREAVES H.W.	MOULDS W. F. *M.M.*	WRIGHT J.T.

After the Second World War the following was added

AND IN MEMORY OF THOSE WHO DIED IN THE 2ND WORLD WAR 1939 1945

DEWEY A. C.	MABBOTT J.W.

THE BRITISH LEGION *John Blundy and John Dewey*

In 1927 a group of ex-servicemen at Hose formed a branch of the British Legion. One of the founder members was Mr E Dewey (father of the Branch Treasurer and Standard Bearer); others were Mr Cheddy Mabbott (Secretary) Mr C Wakefield (Treasurer) and Reverend Bagnall (President). Later Mr E Dewey became President.

Ex-servicemen from Harby joined with the group from Hose and the branch became the Hose and Harby Branch of the British Legion. Members from Harby would include Jim Moulds, Tom Moulds, George Brown and Sam Furmidge.

The Branch holds monthly meetings which alternated between Hose and Harby but more recently have been based in Stathern. These meetings are open to all members where local and national legion business is discussed, fund raising activities organised and welfare reports regarding visits to sick members are given.

In 1969 the condition of the branch standard had deteriorated and a new one was purchased. In 1970 a service of laying up of the old standard and dedication of the new one took place at St Mary's Church, Harby. Lady Martin, president of the Women's Section of the Leicestershire British Legion, was a guest along with standards from branches in Leicestershire. Jim Moulds carried the old standard and John Dewey carried the new one. The Parade Marshall was Mr Tommy Simpkins, Leicestershire Parade Marshal.

The National British Legion was formed in 1921 and to mark the 50th anniversary of The British Legion in 1971 the "Royal" appellation was given by Her Majesty Queen Elizabeth II, patron of the British Legion. The new standard was then reworked to include the word "Royal".

Remembrance services have always taken place at St Mary's Church Harby on Remembrance Sunday morning and before the Chapel closed a service was held there during the afternoon.

British Legion Hose and Harby Branch 1970. Saluting the old and the new Branch standards. Jim Moulds is holding the standard near the camera, John Dewey the far standard. Lady Martin, President of the Women's Section for Leicestershire, stands nearest to the camera. JBLU

Harby life

HARBY ROLL OF HONOUR 1920s to 1946.

In memory of those who died in the Second World War 1939 -1945:

Dewey A C, Mabbott J W.

Men and women of Harby who served and lived through the Second World War:

G A Bremner,	L Mould,
R Buxton,	W Moulds,
B Clark,	K Moulds,
F Cluro,	A Musson,
H Coy,	R Musson,
C L Chambers,	Miss D Musson (ATS),
W Darby,	J Newton,
C Dewey,	J Pepper,
G Furmidge,	Miss A Smith (ATS),
A Hourd,	J Smith,
D Hourd,	K Scarborough,
J Holdsworth,	A Slater,
G Haynes,	Harry Stapleford,
H Haywood,	T Sadler,
J Howitt,	J W Tinsley,
M Howitt,	H Tinsley,
H Howitt,	J Towers,
L Leon,	F Robinson,
A Marston,	B Wilford,
E Manchester,	J Wilford,
F Mabbott,	R Watson,
F Martin,	J Whittle,
	J Wright.

Thomas Lamin served during the 1920s and then in the Home Guard during World War II. Jack Furmidge served from 1925 to 1949.

Post 1946 a number of village men served in the forces either as National Service recruits or on regular engagements and they are still active in the branch.

The school soon after the War Memorial was erected in 1920. The Rev Furnival stands by the Memorial. On the right is Mr Cunnington with two unidentified ladies. NCUN.

Harby: Village life in the Vale of Belvoir

SECOND WORLD WAR

ROYAL OBSERVER CORPS *Rex Stapleford*

In 1947 I was approached by Hector Hallam, the Chief Observer of the Royal Observer Corps (ROC) post at Harby, to see if I would be interested in joining the ROC. Hector was the only one in the post who had served during the war; other wartime members had ceased to be involved when the Second World War finished. They had not been in the forces due to age limitations or being in a reserved occupation, and they had volunteered or were directed to serve in the ROC. During the war the post was manned on a shift basis, day and night. The motto of the ROC was 'forewarned is forearmed'. The Corps stood down on the 12th May 1945, only to be re-activated once more on 1st January 1947. I was only 15 years old at the time, and the minimum age was 16 years, but I claimed to be a year older than I was.

The ROC was established on 25th October 1925 by a committee headed by Major General Romer to provide a co-ordinated early warning system of approaching aircraft and a complementary air defence system. It was at first centred on London. In 1926 it expanded into the Home Counties and up until 1934 new instruments were added to aid observation and dedicated lines of telephone communication installed in the posts.

In 1934 both the ROC and RAF expanded into an integrated home defence air network in Great Britain, incorporating the ROC, the Fighter Command of the RAF and the Chain Home Link Network Radar. By 1939 the ROC was ready and prepared.

The contribution of the ROC during the Second World War years is inestimable. They are undoubtedly the unsung heroes of the time. The Observers' task was to keep track of enemy aircraft and report their movements to a military air defence (fighter) operations centre. They did this through a national network of observation posts sited at vantage points with excellent panoramic views. These posts were sited 5 to 10 miles apart, each reporting to its own Group HQ which fed information directly into an RAF Sector Air Operations Room with an ROC liaison officer. The facts and figures reported were then visually displayed on a plotting board so that RAF controllers would know where to send fighter aircraft to intercept.

The Harby observation post was at first designated J2 (phonetically Jig Two), later changed to F2 (Foxtrot Two), located at the junction of the Hose and Waltham roads. It was a raised square wooden building, with a viewing platform, approximately 10 feet from ground level, surrounded by 4 sides to give wind protection to about shoulder level, but no roof. The viewing platform was reached by a wooden stepladder. There was a covered area at one side of the viewing platform and a storage area underneath. Next to the building was a wooden hut where the aircraft 'spotting' instruments and telephone were stored until required.

The 'spotting' instruments comprised a circular table mounted on a stand at about 4 feet. This was covered in numbered grids relating to Ordnance Survey references and

Harby life

the table was aligned to true north. Apparatus was mounted on the table to provide a means of measuring the height and location of an aircraft within a 5 mile radius of the post. Each of the adjacent posts overlapped in their reporting area. The information was reported by a dedicated telephone line to our Group Centre at Coventry.

A typical report would be:

"J2, 2415, NNW, Junkers 88, 1 at 5 (1000 feet)". This data represented the post number, map grid reference, aircraft direction, aircraft type and height estimation.

At night the aircraft type was replaced by 'heard' and the height and direction estimated from the source of the sound. During transmission of information, voices from the overlapping posts at Bottesford and Wymeswold could be heard.

When I joined in 1947, as well as Hector Hallam, the other members of the post I can recall were Ernie Mumby, Harry Moorehouse and Archie Scott, all from Cropwell Bishop, Bernard Clark from Harby and Graham Richardson from Hose. Hector, Ernie, Harry and Bernard were all employed at A V Roe. Weekly meetings were held at the Nag's Head public house in Harby. Apart from discussions relating to information from Group Headquarters, the main activity during the evening was concerned with aircraft recognition tests. This was carried out by projecting, by an epidiascope, side, front and plan silhouettes of aircraft onto a white screen and photographs of aircraft. After a number of sessions it was remarkable how quickly expertise was achieved in recognizing actual aircraft in flight.

Harby Observer Corps, 1940 by the observation post where Hose Lane leads off from Waltham Road. From left to right: – Back row – Bill Pepper, Tom Wiles, Sam Starbuck, Bob Mackley, Walter Pick, Tom Stokes, Billy Dan Coy, Ernie Martin, Mr Watson. Middle row – Hector Hallam, Arthur Mawson, Tom Dickman, Jack Fairbrother, Billy Coy, Len Pick, Ernie Towers, Eli Coy. Front row – Jim Moulds, Jim Rawlings, Les (Pudding) Whittaker, Mark Curtis, Walter Cook, Mr Williams. The steps leading up to the Observation Post are just showing on the right of the picture. DWHI.

Each year there was a 'Master' aircraft recognition test to achieve the coveted 'Master Aircraft Recognition' badge and find the best Observer at aircraft recognition. There was also a written examination relating to ROC procedures.

During the late 1940s to the mid 1950s, the ROC was involved in joint exercises with the RAF. During these exercises, which usually took place over a weekend, the post was manned full time day and night. Aircraft activity during these exercises was high, and simulated a wartime situation. It was this period of my service in the ROC that gave me the greatest amount of pleasure, since it involved mostly aircraft recognition. There was plenty of aircraft activity locally at the weekends, since 504 Squadron Royal Auxiliary Air Force was sited at RAF Wymeswold from April 1949. During this period all the other local airfields at Newton, Syerston, and Cottesmore were fully manned.

During the 'Cold War' when nuclear warfare was a possibility, it was decided that the main role of the ROC was to monitor radioactive fallout and all posts were located underground. In the late 1950s the wooden tower at Harby was replaced by a concrete structure, and in addition an underground bunker was built. At this point I started to lose interest and eventually ceased to be a member. Apart from my two years' National Service in the RAF, my total service in the ROC at Harby was from 1947 to about 1956.

The post was put on amber alert in the 1961 Cuban missile crisis. Following adverse defence estimates in 1968 many posts were closed. Although much reduced, the organisation continued to train and practise for events it was thankfully never called to act on.

A poem by an anonymous Observer during the Second World War goes as follows:

> At the sky we stare by day and night,
> To identify and plot unwelcome guests,
> And with each speck we observe and ask,
> Did we get that bloody aircraft right?

O-ORANGE REMEMBERED
Dora Butcher from "207 squadron RAF Langar" page 59.

My husband Jack was for several years Secretary of the Harby Village Institute. This used to put on functions for 207 Squadron personnel, such as dances and whist drives, all for sixpence. The hall would be an RAF blue mass. Dancing was almost impossible, four square yards at the most. The music was supplied by gramophone, or local farmers playing the piano and drums (in great demand around the villages of Melton Mowbray).

One evening, Jack was working in the lane, when a young airman came by walking a bike. Jack spoke to him and remarked on his flat tyre. The airman said that he was on his way to Stathern to take some books back. He had no puncture kit so he couldn't repair his tyre. My husband offered to fix it for him. When he called in on the way back, we invited him in for supper. His name was Arthur Archer - he was the Bomb Aimer on

Harby life

Bremner's crew - such a nice chap. After that, he often called in for a chat. He spoke of his parents and girlfriend down in Chingford, Essex and gave us their address if we ever wanted to contact them.

We heard the explosion when O-Orange crashed. We were stunned and shocked when we found out later that it was our friend Arthur's aircraft.

Such was the force of the explosion that four members of the crew were never found and are listed as having no known grave. Arthur Archer was one of them. We had only known him for such a short time but he had become dear to us.

After the accident, I wrote to his parents and invited them up to see for themselves where it happened. They both arrived with Arthur's girlfriend and stayed several days. After the war they asked us down to stay with them and we had a lovely week. They took us to many places of interest, such as Windsor. But sadly, we lost touch as the years went by. We always remember Arthur with great fondness.

PERSONAL MEMORIES OF LANGAR AIRFIELD AND A V ROE - THE SECOND WORLD WAR 1939 - 1945 *Rex Stapleford*

My dad was killed in a road accident in 1941 while serving in the Royal Air Force, which led to my mother and siblings moving to live with her father Sam Furmidge, at Bridge House on Langar Lane. I lived at Ab Kettleby with friends of my father's father, and came to Harby for the school holidays. My first memories of Langar airfield go back to Christmas 1941, when work on the airfield was already underway. The design was the standard for the period with three main runways, the main one on a north-south axis. The majority of the airfield was in the parish of Langar but the southern part was in Harby parish.

During the school holidays, I was afforded a grandstand view of events as my bedroom directly faced the airfield. The airfield opened with No 5 Group Bomber Command, and was first used as a satellite for 207 Squadron, RAF Bottesford, which at that time were equipped with Avro Manchester twin-engine bombers. In September 1942, A V Roe & Co Ltd opened an aircraft repair depot on the west side of the airfield, and they carried out major repairs and reconditioning of Lancasters during the war years. About the same time, No.207 Squadron transferred from Bottesford, by this time flying Avro Lancasters, a four-engine version of the Manchester.

Between September 1942 and September 1943, 207 Squadron took part in many major raids, and I used to watch the aircraft taxiing to the runway and one-by-one taking off on bombing raids during the late evening and returning early in the morning. One of these raids was the bombing of Peenemünde on the evening of the 17th of August 1943. This involved bombing the V1/V2 experimental rocket site located on the Baltic coast of Germany. Nine aircraft of 207 Squadron were involved and they all returned to Langar safely. On this particular raid the RAF lost 44 aircraft and the Luftwaffe 12 aircraft.

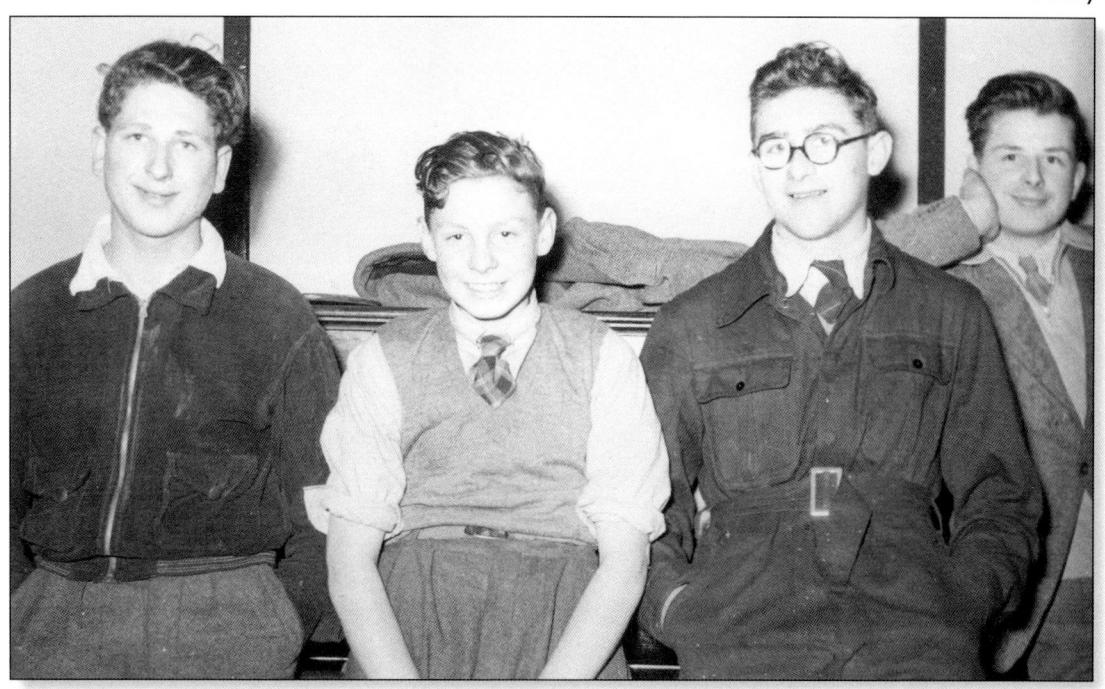

In the Village Institute 1947/48, from left to right Claude Foster, Alec Coy, Trevor Coy and Rex Stapleford. RSTA.

On the night of 3rd of September 1943, Ken Letford and his crew took Wynford Vaughan-Thomas and BBC sound engineer Reg Pidsley to Berlin in their Lancaster ED586, F-Freddie. The Air Officer Commanding No. 5 Group told Vaughan-Thomas "All we ask you to do is to describe what you see. No window dressing." Ken Letford and his crew were not only to bring their two passengers back safely but also shoot down a German nightfighter during the trip, dramatically described in what is now a historic recording.

On the evening of 2nd of October 1943, a Lancaster DV184 (EM-O), the second in the flight of 11 aircraft, crashed during take off in a field on the edge of the airfield and exploded, killing all seven of the crew. The total aircraft losses of 207 Squadron during their time at Langar was 38, the one mentioned above, two lost on crash landing and the remaining 35 lost on operations. Dora and Jack Butcher from Harby befriended Arthur Archer, the bomb aimer, and Dora has left an account of the incident in this book.

In October 1943, the American 9th Air Force took over the airfield from 207 Squadron which moved to RAF Spilsby in Lincolnshire. The station became No. 490 of the 9th Air Force.

Various TCG's (Troop Carrier Groups), equipped with Douglas Dakota transport and glider towing aircraft, were stationed at Langar and initially the airfield was used as a reception base and for training these groups, before they moved South to prepare for

D-Day. It also assembled and modified Waco CG-4A gliders. The Americans left Langar in late September 1944, shortly after 45 Dakota C47 aircraft were used to drop 1,922 American paratroopers at Nijmegen in Holland for their contribution to the 'Market Garden' operation. This was followed by a series of reinforcement operations carried out from Langar, in the form of C47s towing gliders. For the Market Garden operation some of the paratroopers were accommodated in tents adjacent to the hangar nearest to Harby.

My brother Peter and my sisters Anne and Jean went to the children's Christmas party given by the Americans in 1943, and they were all presented with a small bible. I went to see the film 'Jane Eyre' at the camp cinema in the summer holidays of 1944, with my Aunt Marion Furmidge. The huts housing the American airmen were sited on the west side of the road, past Gale's Farm.

During the time that the Americans were at Langar my mother laundered clothes for two American airmen who were Master Sergeants. Apart from providing some income for the family they often brought chocolates (which of course were on ration in Great Britain) and tins of fruit.

After the Americans left, between October 1944 and March 1945, Langar became the home of 1669 Heavy Conversion Unit with Lancasters and Halifax bombers. After they left the airfield was exclusively used by A V Roe, until the Royal Canadian Air Force came in 1952.

JAM AND JERUSALEM
Harby Women's Institute from "Minutes in Time" pages 65 -72.

Jam and the WI are probably forever linked - and why not? It is very satisfying to turn surplus fruit from your own or a friend's garden into a shelf full of well set jars of jam.

During the war Harby WI members made jam - a great deal of jam. When the programme for 1939 was being assembled "no one seemed keen on having a lecture on jams and jellies" but when the war was but a few weeks old, that is what the members got and not long after classes were under way.

Although rationing had not yet started, an allocation of sugar had been obtained for these classes. Not all the sugar was used and in the following year it was noted that "sugar left over from the distribution for classes on fruit preservation to be kept for use at WI". The next item in the minutes suggests just what this spare sugar was to be used for – "tea was to be bought before rationing starts" - so the cup of tea at the end of meetings was safeguarded for the time being!

In the war years the production of Stilton cheese was suspended, such luxuries were low on the list of priorities. Theoretically this left Mrs. Watson with more free time but in reality it gave her the opportunity to devote her considerable energies to the wartime effort. The United Dairy run by Mr. Herbert Watson was at the heart of the village in more than just the geographical sense. Centrally placed on a triangle of land, now bordered on two sides by Watsons Lane, named in recognition of the considerable contribution to the community made by the Watsons, it provided much needed employment and formed an important part in the lives of many village families.

In the spring of 1940 arrangements for setting up a co-operative fruit preservation centre were under way. Those wanting to join had made their application for sugar to the secretary and "all ration books were signed and stamped for permits" for it. Mrs. Musson seems very pleased to have a special stamp: "We shall all find it very useful" she writes.

Meanwhile the committee appointed the officers to run the centre. Mrs. Watson was made chairman and chief controller, Mrs. Dickman secretary and Miss Moulds the "lady in charge". All the other committee members were to help. They decided to put in a bulk order for "7 cwts of sugar for autumn fruit" and to ask members to bring jam jars and stoves for "cooking jam". Fourteen stoves were promised, presumably paraffin ones as these would have been portable. Joan Watson recalls the use of the dairy for this large scale task with the jam being stored on the temporarily empty cheese store shelves.

Sixty people had given their names as "wanting or willing to make jam", each was allocated 12-13 lbs of sugar and they were to start "at 2.00 p.m. on Thursday" in late August. In the following month, the minutes record that "jam making to be continued .... with the new allowance of sugar approximately 5 lbs per household". In October, "2,128 lbs of jam were distributed to members of the centre" - nearly a ton!

The Women's Volunteer Service children's mobile kitchen van, presented by the Kiwanis Club of Vancouver to the Save the Children Fund, outside the school in 1942. CBOO.

Harby life

In common with other preservation centres around the country, a letter thanking them for their efforts was received from Lord Woolton, the Minister of Food, this with one from Lady Denman, National Chairman of the WI "on the same subject" was read out to members.

The garden of Dairy House produced all manner of fruit and vegetables and dairy workers helped with its upkeep during slack times. Mr. Tom Moulds cared for the garden followed later by Mr. Jim Moulds. Parsnips for wine, excellent celery and masses of tomatoes which were bottled for future use, grew alongside the fruit housed in a cage. Loganberries, raspberries and strawberries were mostly used for jam. The surplus produce from the garden, apart from the wartime use, contributed to many a fund raising effort. From 1941 on the running of the centre must have become routine and the only way of knowing it continued is from the annual reports of the election of officers and appeals for jam jars.

Jam making was not the only thing the WI did to help the war effort. On hearing a talk on the importance of "camouflage work", thirty-six members volunteered to do it, while others attended lectures in Melton to learn how to do general repairs, plumbing and electrical work. They distributed parcels of clothes for evacuees in 1940 and for members' children in 1946. They attended "make do and mend" classes, where maybe they learned how to make a pencil skirt from a pair of men's dress trousers or a small child's dress from the tails of an otherwise worn out shirt.

They formed a knitting group who met weekly, making scarves, socks and pullovers for "our boys in the forces". Wool for such things could be purchased without coupons and they set up a wool fund in 1941 for the purpose. Mr. Price organized a darts match to raise money for the wool fund and sent a donation. They also knitted shawls from an allocation of wool they received.

As well as her WI commitments, Mrs. Watson was involved in other work to help the war effort, like the Land Army and nursing but she will be remembered by many for her exceptional achievement in raising enough money to give £18, a substantial sum of money, to each serviceman from Harby returning home after the war. The Harby Boys' Comfort Fund record book detailing the funds raised with some of the letters of thanks is a testament to her skills. In later years, when incapacitated, she frequently asked "Am I being useful?". Her whole life had been spent being "useful" and inspiring others to be useful too.

Members made "searchlight curtains for Cropwell Bishop" and started a War Savings Group in the WI. In 1942 after making a "special effort" they proudly announced that they had saved "£500 during the year". Savings stamps were given as prizes for games and competitions at monthly meetings.

Mrs. Watson's office became a depot every Monday afternoon, where mothers would come to collect the free orange juice, cod liver oil and baby milk which was allocated to their children. Members also manned the desks when old ration books were collected and new ones issued. The WI also distributed Harby's share of the cocoa and dried milk mixture sent from Canada for all British children, some readers may remember how delicious this was.

They grew vegetables from seed obtained cheaply from the county office who bought in bulk from Suttons. The onion club was "not a very successful venture", though they did manage to collect 77 lbs together for a Red Cross appeal. The onions were destined for men on minesweepers.

Nobody was keen to gather and dry nettles, but they were happy to collect rose hips as well as to dry mint and parsley. For these they received some payment which was donated to the Harby Boys' Comfort Fund. This fund was also supplemented by some of the dances organised by the WI. On average they ran four a year for various causes, also several whist drives. These events must have helped keep up the spirits of the whole community throughout the war.

Stilton cheese production was eventually restored after the war.

AFTER THE WAR

LANGAR AIRFIELD AND INDUSTRIAL ESTATE 1945 TO 1975
Rex Stapleford

When the war in Europe came to an end in June 1945, I moved to live with the rest of my family in Harby. My mother and I went to a dance during the summer holidays in 1945 held in one of the ex-RAF buildings across the road from A V Roe. The band members were German Prisoners of War, rather incongruously playing Glenn Miller type music.

It was in 1945 that the then unknown author Alan Sillitoe was posted to Langar as an assistant air traffic control officer in the control tower. At the time there were two other assistants, and an RAF Squadron Leader in charge. One of the assistants stayed at the Police House on Stathern Lane. Alan Sillitoe resigned from his post at Langar about March 1946. His autobiography describes how he travelled to work on the A V Roe workers' special buses from Nottingham.

I left school in July 1946 and started work as an apprentice at A V Roe, as did Ron Lamin from Harby and Geoff Daft from Hose. I remember catching the bus across the road from Bridge House and that my overalls were too long in the leg and were turned up at the bottoms to allow for my continuing growth. For the first two years the working week was five and a half days, and my starting wage was 26 shillings per week. The Works Superintendent was Mr Phil Lightfoot, who after the war played cricket for Harby. His daughter Anne subsequently married local farmer's son Tom Swingler, who also played for the cricket team.

In the Very Long Range hangar near Barnstone on the Langar airfield in 1947/1948, Lincoln bombers undergoing repairs. RSTA.

Major overhaul work was carried out on three aircraft types, the Lancaster and Lincoln bombers, and the York transport. In addition, conversions from military to civilian use were carried out. The works comprised Shed Nos. 1-7, and when I started work they also used four T1-type hangars on the airfield. One hangar, just over the road from the main works, was used to prepare aircraft for flight testing. Another hangar was located on the Harby side of the airfield. The other two were located on the Barnstone side of the airfield and were referred to as VLR (Very Long Range) because of the proposed fitment of additional 'saddle' fuel tanks in the bomb bays of Avro Lincoln bombers.

My first job was in Shed 5 involving wrapping asbestos string around oil pipes on the Rolls Royce Merlin XX engines fitted to the Lancaster bomber. Then I was moved to Shed 1 to work on the 'Engine Sub Frame' Section.

During the time I was in Shed 1, I was involved in an accident that could have cost me my life. During the mid-morning break, while fetching tea from the canteen for the others, I was run over by a three-wheel vehicle. The driver's view was shielded from the side exit of the hangar by a toilet block built at the side of the hangar. I was taken to the Nottingham City Hospital, and was away from work for a few weeks recuperating. A barrier was put up to stop anyone running straight out of the hangar and all vehicles were sent in the opposite direction. After returning to work following my accident I suffered a little from fainting fits, attributed to the delayed shock of the accident and I was transferred to working in the VLR hangars. The majority of this was the major overhauls of the Lincoln bomber.

In 1948 the Russians closed all the rail and road links into Berlin. All essential supplies to the British, American and French sectors had to be ferried by air. On June 23rd 1948, operation 'Plainfare' got underway, and the RAF used 40 Yorks which carried the bulk of the British contribution. These used to fly into Langar for overhaul, with traces of coal and flour covering the passenger compartment (with all seats removed). I remember standing outside one of the VLR hangars watching a York flying in from Germany, and saying to one of my colleagues that 'it seems to be going slow'. This was followed by an inevitable stall, and a heavy landing on one wheel, with a resultant collapsed undercarriage and the aircraft veering off the runway.

We had three famous York aircraft at Langar in 1946/47. Firstly, LV633 'Ascalon' was the aircraft used by Winston Churchill and sometimes King George VI. It had square windows, not the normal round ones. We also had the Yorks of General de Gaulle and the Duke of Gloucester, when he was the Governor of Australia. Quite a few Yorks were converted at Langar from military to civilian use for airlines such as British South American Airways and Skyways.

The Chief Test Pilot at Langar was Squadron Leader Peter Field-Richards; he could probably do more spectacular flying manoeuvres with Lancasters, Lincolns and Yorks than most pilots. During 1947, I had my second ever flight in an aeroplane with Peter in a Lancaster, mainly flying over Nottingham. His particular stunt after most flights was to beat up the airfield and pull the stick back to climb for a wingtip turn. This was a most unpleasant experience at the time for a young lad. Peter and his wife Jessie were also the landlords of the Nag's Head pub in Harby.

Peter was born in 1910 and had been in the army before serving in the RAF. He had got his pilot's licence in 1929. He also raced cars and aeroplanes before the Second World War. In the early days of A V Roe at Langar he was posted in as the Test Pilot. When the Americans arrived at Langar, Peter was told that they had never towed gliders before. So one morning he showed the two Flight Commanders how it was done and that afternoon they were instructing their own pilots. There are quite a few anecdotes concerning Peter. It is said that he regularly borrowed an American Dakota (C47) to get home for the weekend. At that time his wife was living in Christchurch, Hampshire. When the Americans left Langar they cleared out their stores and gave chickens, tinned fruit, chocolates and sweets to the local villagers. Peter was the recipient of cigars and cigarettes, which was enough to last him for two years.

Neil Cunnington standing by the last Shackleton WL798 to fly from Langar airfield on 4 September 1968. NCUN.

Harby life

Langar airfield about 1946. In the foreground is an Avro Lincoln bomber, under its wing in the distance an Avro York transport aircraft. JBLU.

A few months before I left AV Roe in March 1950, I was transferred back to the main site working exclusively on the York aircraft. The future of the aircraft repair depot at Langar was bleak in January 1950 when it was expected to close down within the next six months owing to lack of contracts. Some 750 people were on the staff then. However civilian contracts were negotiated and about a year later work began preparing the airfield as an air materials base for the Royal Canadian Air Force. No. 30 Air Material Base moved in during October 1952. The site comprised 44 buildings, 25 being new. The domestic site had 11 buildings with the Personnel Married Quarters site situated at Radcliffe-on-Trent.

The Canadians were very much liked in the Nottinghamshire countryside and towns and became an integral part of the Nottinghamshire community. In 1960 a maple tree was planted in Granby, presented by the people of Granby, Quebec. For 11 years the base throbbed with life, then, in 1963 RCAF Langar, which had spread over 377 acres, closed down. Three years later the Canadians left. In September 1968 A V Roe closed down. The post-war years had seen Avro Yorks, Lancastrians, Shackletons and Gloster Meteors pass through the establishment.

In the 28 years, from inception up to the closure of AV Roe, Langar Airfield provided employment for many of the local villages, plus many from Nottingham and Melton Mowbray. When I worked at A V Roe there used to be at least a dozen double-deck buses from Nottingham, picking up people en-route. One bus returned to Nottingham with the drivers, returning at finishing time to take the workers home.

The canteen ladies at A V Roe works on Langar airfield in the early 1950s. On the back row from the left third is Belle Stapleford, ninth Mrs Walter Wilkinson. On the front row from the left are second "Dick" Prichett the Deputy Manageress, third Mrs Grinnel the Manageress. RSTA.

Harby: Village life in the Vale of Belvoir

3. THE SCHOOL

THE EARLY SCHOOL *Leslie Cram*

The deeds of Dove Cottage in Dickmans Lane give the earliest written evidence of schools in Harby. They record that in 1796 it became a Dame School where there was a lady who took in young children to give them simple education. The brick single storey building next to the house was the schoolroom. Peggy Shipman remembers that a three year old child paid two pence a week.

The present Harby Church of England Primary School began from the initiative of the National Society for Promoting Religious Education in the whole of the country. It was founded by the Rector about 1827, the exact date is not recorded, with the land given by the Duke of Rutland. The trade directory for 1846 tells us that the school master then was William Burnham. The 1851 census records the school master as William Chandler, his wife Emma being the school mistress.

Harby School from the south, around 1915. The "tin school", a temporary building put up to take the more than average numbers of children at this time, is shown in the playground. POBR

The Record Office for Leicestershire, Leicester and Rutland holds two documents from 1856 which set out the plans for rebuilding the school. The first is the architect's drawing of the new building with separate playgrounds and school rooms for boys and girls and accommodation for the school master and his family. This is the building we can see today. The second is the conveyance document referring to the land "given by me (Duke of Rutland) as Lord of the Manor as and for a site for a school for the said parish on or about the year 1827 but of which no conveyance has ever been executed". The document goes on to state that the new building is – "to be used as and for a school for the education of children and adults or children only of the labouring manufacturing and other poor classes in the parish of Harby". It says that the school is to be open to inspection by government inspectors and operated under the National Society for Promoting the Education of the Established Church. Details of how it will be governed are set out with a committee of management composed of village people. There was a

Harby life

new certificated school master, Henry Major, aged 23, born in Folkestone. The 1863 trade directory sums it up "The National School is a handsome stone building, erected in 1860, at a cost of nearly £1000, raised by subscription and grants. It is attended by about 90 children."

Log books of school activities and minute books of the school governors exist as far back as 1863. Here is an extract from the 1863 – 1901 log book kept in the Record Office for Leicestershire, Leicester and Rutland reference E/LB/136/1.

1899

June 5th. Children photographed today by Mr Perks, of Melton Mowbray and Kettering.

June 12th. Half-holiday this afternoon owing to Wesleyan Sunday School Treat.

June 15th. M E Starbuck away from school today, with bad cold. Time table not strictly adhered to.

June 16th. M E Starbuck returned to work this morning. Attendance very fair – older scholars still attending very badly.

June 19th. Several test examinations in Arithmetic, Spelling and Composition will be given this week.

June 22nd. Wet morning – Attendance dropped through it. Half-holiday this afternoon, owing to most of the Standard children going to Belvoir in connection with the Band of Hope of this village.

June 23rd. Owing to the continued wet, the half-holiday was not given yesterday but today instead.

June 26th. Attendance much larger today than usual.

Inside Harby school about 1950. From left to right the children are Julia Brown, Marion Mackley, Celia Tomlinson, Valerie Leon and Sam Towers. A poster for BBC broadcasts to schools of this period is in the background and the measuring tape for how fast the children were growing. Sam's socks have slipped down to his ankles. BTOW.

Harby life

Harby School, showing a youthful Mr Edwards soon after he came to the school in 1886. A count gives some 90 children and 4 teachers. JWAT.

Harby school in 1895. Taken from School Lane with the teachers and pupils in front of the school building. Behind the children on the right are five teachers, Mr Edwards on the left, Matilda Musson, then three lady teachers whose names are not known. A count of the number of children gives 121. POBR.

Harby: Village life in the Vale of Belvoir

Harby life

Harby school 1912, in the playground. The board reads Harby 1912 ALL III. From left to right: on the back row Mr Edwards on the extreme right, second row 4th from left Annie Ward, unidentified, May Rawlings, unidentified, Dorothy Ward, Olive Mary Furmidge, front row extreme right Madge Rawlings. The girls are mostly dressed in loose white dresses with lace around the neck and boots or heavy shoes. The boys often have a white Eton collar. POBR.

Harby school about 1925. From left to right - Back row – Alec Moulds, Blackwell, Ward, Olive Whittle, Nance White, Freda Fairbrother, unknown, Bailey. Middle row – Miss Edith Buxton, ? Sam Furmidge, Furmidge, Blackwell, Wilford, Winifred Stokes, Cliff Wilford, Annie Howitt, Howitt, Ellis White, Mr Edwards. Front row - Bilby, Whittle, Howitt, unidentified, Phyllis Mackley, Wilford, ? Blackwell. POBR.

Harby: Village life in the Vale of Belvoir

Harby life

School group about 1946, Burden Lane in the background with Oakhurst on the right. From left to right on the front row is Anne Tinsley, Jennifer Seal, Ann Hilsden, Brenda Foster, Wendy Coy, Sheila Manchester, Sheila Kemp, Kathleen Beet; back row - Colin Slater, Winston Rawlings, Ron Grove, Derek Foster, Tony Hewitt, John Mackley, Neil Cunnington, Michael Hall, Peter Groves, Alan Martin. JMAC.

Harby school 1960 looking over School Lane. From left to right - Back row – Eric Lane, Mary Tinsley, unidentified, Richard Thomlinson, unidentified, Cheryl Thorpe, Ron Slater, John Hourd, Linda Moulds, Linda Slater, unidentified, Glyn Holdsworth, Mrs Pearson. Middle row – Gillian Dewey, David Eatherington, Stuart Pymm, unidentified, June Holdsworth, unidentified, Bernard Palmer, Ann Hallam, Howard Dawson, Mary Hallam, unidentified. Front seated – unidentified, Christopher Dames, Pam Tinsley, unidentified, Hourd twins, Andrew Osborne, Tony Shipman, Ian Dawson. Front on ground – Jane Wright, unidentified, unidentified, Michael Whittle, unidentified, Robert Tinsley, Patsy Partridge, Jane Dewey, Wendy Whittle, unidentified. BTOW.

Harby: Village life in the Vale of Belvoir

Harby life
THE CONSTRUCTION AND MANAGEMENT OF HARBY SCHOOL
Neil Cunnington

The school was built in 1860, on the old village green, by a Church committee, headed by the Rev. M. O. Norman, and was opened 25th March, 1861. Two sermons were preached by the Rev. James Barsdsley, Rector of St. Ann's Church, Manchester, on behalf of the school building fund, in the Parish Church on Wednesday, September 25th 1861, at 11am and 3pm. The surveyors and architects were Bellamy and Hardy of Lincoln, whose plans were approved by the Rev. Norman, John Morrison and George Chester.

COST
Original Contract	£560 2s 6d
Extras	£141 8s 3d
Stone getting and cutting	£ 31 19s 0d
Sundries	£ 71 15s 9d
Architect	£ 55 17s 10d
	£861 3s 4d

RECEIPT
Subscriptions raised in Parish	£253 13s 0d
Extras paid for by Rev. M.O. Norman	£141 8s 3d
Sale of old school	£ 12 13s 6d
Collection Sept. 26th 1860	£ 29 2s 1d
Sundries	£ 45 1s 1d
National Society	£ 30 0s 0d
Government grant	£290 0s 0d
To Balance	£ 59 5s 5d
	£861 3s 4d

The school was large enough to accommodate 120 children but the average attendance was only 80. The first headmaster was Mr. Henry Major. The County Council took over the management of the school on July 1st 1903.

The new school viewed from the road when newly built in 1860. On the left appears to be the Rector, standing as he is shown in photograph on page 166. CBOO.

MR EDWARDS *Leslie Cram*

Mr Alfred Warman Edwards, the school headmaster, came from London and married a local Harby girl from the Furmidge family, a relative of Barbara Stead. He came to the school as a temporary appointment for 3 weeks and the post became permanent. He is first listed in the school logbooks in 1886. He resigned from the post on April 6 1926. After he retired he lived in Wharflands on Colston Lane then moved to a bungalow in Pinfold Lane. As well as teaching children during the day he ran a night school for adults in the school rooms. He would write letters for those who could not write themselves. After the village hall or village institute opened in 1922 he became the head of the committee. It was overwhelmingly for men, with a billiard table in the kitchen which had boards placed over it when food was being prepared, and facilities for darts, dominoes and ping pong. He became a lay reader in the church, taking services which included reading sermons composed by others but not preaching himself. He was secretary to the owner of Harby Mill, Mr Stubbs.

Mr Edwards the school headmaster, about 1900 with unidentified lady on the left and the infant teacher Matilda Musson on the right. CBOO.

An oil painting by Guilford Wood of the church in 1921 viewed from the south west. The stone wall can be seen along the north side of the churchyard, the left of the picture. LCRA

4. THE CHURCH

GRAVEYARD VERSES

The inscriptions on gravestones sometimes include poetry. Here are the two favourite ones chosen by the Church Warden, Henry Clark, who surveyed the churchyard and recorded them all. The survey is to be seen on the website www.harby.co.uk/churchyard.htm, in the church and in the Record Office for Leicestershire, Leicester and Rutland.

Grave 163. Thomas Francis, who died aged 22 in 1716.

> Reader stand still and lend a tear
> Upon the dust that sleepeth here
> And whilst thou read the state of me
> Think on the glass that runs for thee.

Grave 198. Benjamin Hargrave, who died aged 65 in 1784.

> Farewell vain World, I've had enough of thee,
> Nor do I care what thou canst say of Me;
> Thy Smiles I court not nor thy frowns I fear
> All's one to me, my head lies quiet here:
> What faults thou'st seen in me, take care to shun
> Look thou at Home, enough there's to be done.

HISTORY OF HARBY CHURCH *Rev M O Norman*

Reverend M O Norman was rector of Harby from October 2 1852 to his death on May 28 1899. During this time the church was restored. From his observations during the restoration Rev. Norman wrote a brief history of the building kept in the Record Office for Leicestershire, Leicester and Rutland reference number DE 3489/3, dated January 1877.

An engraving of the church in 1874 just before restoration. CBOO.

Harby life

Originally it consisted of small nave and chancel – both of which had high pitched roofs and was without tower, clerestory or aisles or porch. The original pitch of the nave roof may still be traced inside the church on the wall above the chancel arch and the pitch of the chancel by the end of the weather moulding outside the chancel which may be seen on both sides of the chancel close to where it joins onto the nave. The chancel in this form was built in what is known as the early English style of architecture and was probably completed in the reign of Henry III who began to reign in the year 1216. After this the following changes took place. First the chancel was altered, the walls were raised and high windows were put in, the east window belongs to that style of architecture called the decorated and was put up certainly by not later than the reign of Edward III who reigned from 1327 – 1377. Somewhat later the tower was built and stood as a separate building as may be inferred from the fact that it has buttresses at the four corners and is joined on to the nave without any stones connecting the one to the other. The body of the nave was taken down and was rebuilt with arches and a clerestory above and aisles, the aisles being joined on, as may be still seen, somewhat clumsily to the ends of the nave which were left standing. These last changes which brought the chancel into this state were probably completed not later than 1450 in the reign of Henry VI and from that time no change of any importance was made until the late work of restoration. We are therefore worshipping where our ancestors for six hundred years have worshipped before us, there they were baptised and married and around which "the forefathers of the Hamlet sleep".

Harby St Mary's Church in 1904, seen from the east with the new vestry which was added in 1903. NCUN.

Harby life

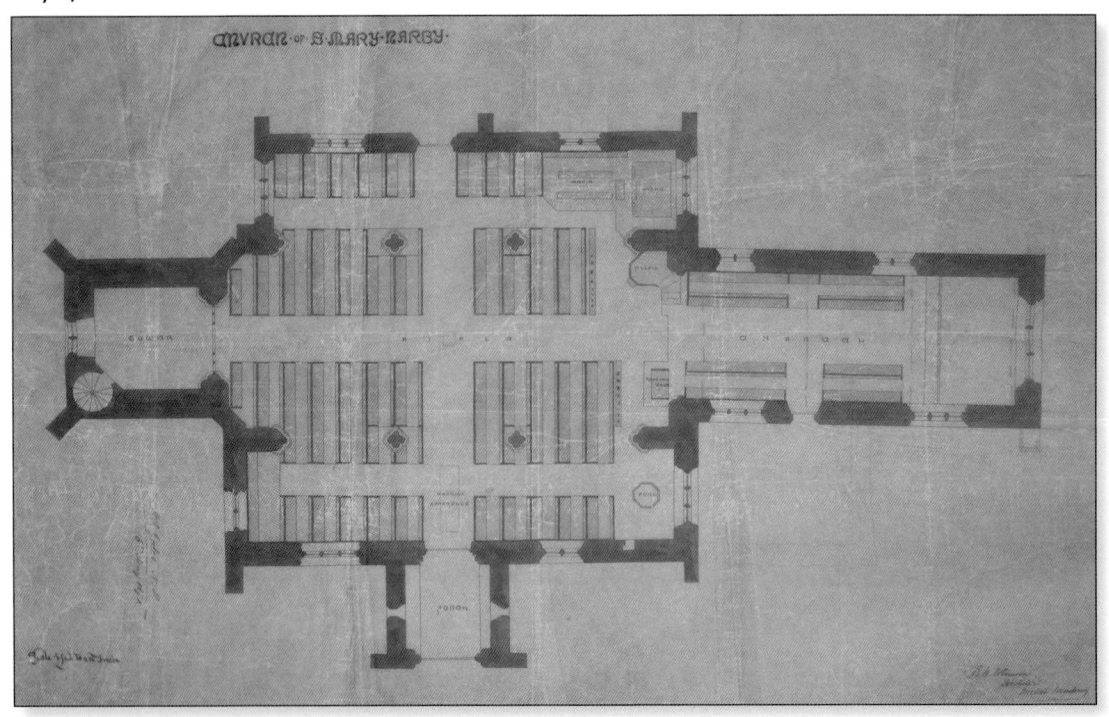

Plan of the Church of St Mary Harby, drawn in 1874 for the restoration work by B K Musson, Architect, Melton Mowbray. Scale one foot to an inch. It shows the organ at the east end of the north aisle with the choir seats beside it. The font is at the east end of the south aisle. The plan clearly shows the slight angle there is between the axis of the nave and the chancel. Image supplied by the Record Office for Leicestershire, Leicester and Rutland reference number DE 1772/48. Reproduced by kind permission of the Parochial Church Council. PCC.

Inside the church looking east along the nave, after the restoration of 1875. The servants and it is thought the family from the Rectory sat in the chancel seats. The choir sat on the left behind the low curtains. The organ is on the left at the east end of the north aisle. The front of the nave has chairs not pews as now. The pews were made by the village carpenter. A double oil lamp hangs in front of the chancel. One of the globes of another such lamp can be seen in the top right. CBOO.

HARBY PARISH ALMANACK 1888

The Church Almanack for 1888 includes a letter from the Rector:-

Mr Dear Friends,

Again, at the commencement of a New Year, I address you. The year 1887 will always be remarkable as the Jubilee year of our Sovereign, who has reigned longer than any of her predecessors except two — Henry III (1216-1272) and George III (1760 - 1820). We may very truly conclude that we have abundant reason to thank God for a Sovereign, under whose rule an Empire such as ours, has enjoyed the peace and quietness which has marked her fifty years of reign.

It is a matter of much congratulation that, by the hearty co-operation of all classes in the parish, we have added one as a Jubilee Bell to our peal, and have put the whole peal on a new frame;—a work which those who saw the old frame will readily acknowledge was much needed. I wish that the pleasant invitation which they ring out from Sabbath to Sabbath was more largely responded to - I wish all could respond to the lines:

Sabbath! blessed day of rest;
Holy Sabbath, Heavenly Sabbath,
Of the seven I love thee best !
Holy Sabbath, Heavenly Sabbath.

Hark! thy Bells are sounding clear,
Holy Sabbath, Heavenly Sabbath,
Sweet their music to mine ear:
Holy Sabbath, Heavenly Sabbath.

Depend upon it, the habitual neglect of public worship on God's holy day is a habit full of danger to the soul. Some people tell me they can just as well serve God on the Sabbath reading their book in their own room, I venture to say that this is only one of the manifold delusions with which the Devil — too successfully, alas! —endeavours to beguile souls. I ask any one to read Luke iv, 6 and Acts xvii, 2, and consider whether it can be safe to cast to the winds two such examples as are there set before us.

In the beginning of the world, God ordained two, and only two, institutions — the Sabbath and Marriage, as fences to prevent men from making all things common; and I regret to note that there are many who break down the fence and scruple not to disregard it.

In respect to these two most important matters, I conclude with two passages from God's Word —

"Ye shall keep my Sabbaths, and reverence my Sanctuary: I am the Lord". — Lev. xxvi.

"Wherewithal shall a young man, or woman, cleanse their way? By taking heed thereto according to Thy word", ' — Ps. cxix

I am. Affectionately yours,

M O NORMAN.

Harby life
COME TO CHURCH LETTER ABOUT 1910

Carrying no date on it and with no signature, a letter was sent out apparently to every parishioner urging the people of Harby to attend church. We give a date of about 1910 and assume it came from the rector of the time, Rev Stone. A copy in the Record Office for Leicestershire, Leicester and Rutland dates it 1910. It has a picture of the church originally published by John Nichols in 1815. This is what it says:-

Harby St. Mary.

Fellow-Christians,

Will you accept this picture of your Parish Church? Harby Church was built in the reign of Henry VII., 1485, and was probably an off-shoot from the Monastic Establishment at Stathern. It was restored in Mr. Norman's time, 1874, and a Vestry was added 1903. Its registers begin abruptly 1700 and the old tradition says "That the Clerk in those days who had charge of the registers wrapped his wife's dead body in them before placing her in her coffin and they were buried with her, because of the old superstition that if you wrapped a dead body in parchment (and the registers were of parchment) it would keep evil spirits away". We have a few old bell-ringing customs — Every Sunday at 8 the bell is rung and finishes with the number of strokes of days in the month - Shrove Tuesday a Pancake bell is rung at 11 a.m. When there is a week-day service at mid-day a bell is rung, called a Sermon bell. At five minutes before ten every week-day an Angelus bell is rung. The Passing bell finishes with 3 for a man and 2 for a woman.

Now, I expect deep down in their hearts everyone in this Village is proud of this beautiful building that for long ages has been the centre of the Worship of God in these surroundings. And from being proud of it as a building, it has some veneration in our eyes as a place of worship. Where men and women for generations have come seeking rest and comfort from God.

Now, we are saying these things, and asking you to accept this picture to hang up in your homes, because we feel the Village is going back from these old ways of God worship. That your Church is gradually being deserted. We want you to help us stop this. We know, because the Bible tells of God's Tabernacle and God's Temple being built by God's command, that it is God's wish that we should meet together to worship Him. So we want you for God's sake to come out again and meet God and one another. Or, on the other hand, if you do worship God in His House, and know all the joy and comfort of that worship to try and get those who have fallen away from the public worship of God to come back again.

Of course you will understand, this in no way refers to those who worship God in Chapel, only so far as it may help them to gather in their own who have turned aside from their God.

We have only one end, one object, one desire, in sending you this letter — that you and I may gain Eternal Life with God.

For after all, when you have summed it all up
"Here we have no continuing city, but we seek one to come."

Harby life

Christmas Fayre in the village hall 1959. From left to right - Ann Lightfoot and baby, Dora Butcher, Mrs Chambers, Mrs Jimmy Moulds, Mrs Tomlinson, Flo Oxbrough, Avis Wright, Mrs Brown, Mrs Ruby Waring, Adela Thomson, Mrs Walker and child, Mrs Mackley. The table is actually the billiard table with boards placed on top. Copyright Melton Times and reproduced here with their kind permission

Church Sunday School annual flower service about 1948, outside the school. From left to right-back row Mr Lane, the headmaster, Anne Stapleford, Jean Stapleford; front row Carole Stapleford. Also Christine Pepper, Sammy Towers, Margaret Gilder, Anne Tinsley. CBOO.

West of the church, Church Rogation Sunday parade at 6.20 pm about 1947. Leading the procession is the Bishop of Leicester, Guy Vernon Smith. Other identifiable people from left to right are - Sheila Hodges, Edith Buxton, Hilda Buxton, Ron Lamin, Mary Hodges, Mrs Lamin, Anne Lightfoot, Jean Stapleford, Nellie Harwood, Pat Buxton, Anne Tinsley, Christine Pepper, Betty Pepper. Rogation processions are from a tradition of asking for blessing on the crops and walking round the boundaries of the village. CBOO.

Harby: Village life in the Vale of Belvoir

Harby life

ST MARY'S CHURCH INCUMBENTS   *Leslie Cram,*

Here is a list of the Rectors in the village from 1700 to 1975. Each played his part in the community, and officiated at the times of transition in the lives of Harby families with the baptism of a new child, marriages and funerals.

John Major 1703 to 1739

William Turvile 1739 to 1741

Samuel Kerchevall 1741 to 1749

Richard Stevens 1749 to 1751

William Cant 1751 to 1763

Bennet Storer 1763 to 1804

Thomas Norris 1804 to 1826

William Evans Hartopp 1826 to 1852

Manners Octavius Norman 1852 to 1899

Edward Henry Stone 1899 to 1925

Arthur Evelyn Furnival 1926 to 1947

William Paul Watkins 1947 to 1949

Alfred Cuthbert Holden 1949 to 1959

Charles Brian Underwood 1960 to 1961

Joseph Henry Dransfield 1962 to 1963

Ieuan Delvin Powell-Hughes 1964 to 1974

John Sydney Savige from 1975

Rev Manners Octavius Norman and his wife about 1875. CBOO.

Rev Stone on the tennis court at the Old Rectory about 1920. FBAN.

Playing bowls on the rectory lawn at the Garden Fete about 1930. From the left are Mrs Annie Herrick, Mrs Mary Ann Kemp and Rev Furnival. NCUN.

134   Harby: Village life in the Vale of Belvoir

Harby life

*Rev. W. P. Watkins in 1949.
Melton Mowbray Times
March 11, 1949.*

Bellringers outside the south porch at Harby church about 1955. From left to right they are - back row - Mac Hoyes, unidentified, Jack Butcher, Noel Wilson, Mr Mackley, George Payne, Reg Pritchett; front row - Bill Sharp, Rev Holden, Ernie Martin. JMAC.

Rev Dransfield in 1963. JBLU.

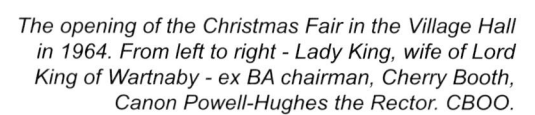

The opening of the Christmas Fair in the Village Hall in 1964. From left to right - Lady King, wife of Lord King of Wartnaby - ex BA chairman, Cherry Booth, Canon Powell-Hughes the Rector. CBOO.

In the Village Hall about 1975. On the left Mrs Savige with Rev Savige beside her. JBLU.

Harby: Village life in the Vale of Belvoir 135

Harby life

5. THE CHAPEL

HISTORY OF HARBY METHODIST CHAPEL

Nora Blaze from material kindly lent by Miss B. Stead, from Harby News issue 7 pages 18 to 20.

The month of May 1929 saw a red-letter day in Harby, for it marked the centenary of the Methodist Chapel. The original chapel was a coachhouse, given for the purpose by Mr William Orson in April 1828. It was made into a comfortable place of worship, and services took place there for nearly twenty years. Mr Orson preached the first sermon.

On the formation of the Methodist society, Mrs Orson was appointed to the office of class leader. Prior to 1828 Wesleyan Methodism had no existence in the village. A short time previously the Primitive Methodists had visited Harby and formed a small society. When Mr and Mrs Orson came to live here they began a cause connected with the Wesleyans, not in opposition to the Primitives, but one which they deemed to be more in harmony with their own religious views and feelings. This arrangement was followed by the Primitive Methodists discontinuing their services and amalgamating with the Methodists.

The Methodist chapel about 1930. FBAN.

The first mention of Harby in the circuit books was in December 1829, when the sum of 18/- was recorded as the quarterage. In 1830 the first record of names was given: Ann Orson (leader), William Orson, Sarah Rose, George Hall, John Richards, Sarah Wesson, Richard Knapp, Mary Starbuck, Sarah Knapp, Mary Harriman, Milley Rose, John Orson, Ann Stafford, and Elizabeth Brian. The leader was a most devoted Christian, and an active and intelligent woman. In her younger days she stood firm and faithful to Methodism amidst persecution and reproach and in her will she left £1 for every local preacher whose name was on the Melton Mowbray plan.

The congregation having outgrown the coachhouse, a new place of worship was needed, so in 1847 the village chapel was built on Mr Orson's land. The foundation stone was laid by Mr C H Clarke, a Nottingham solicitor, and the opening sermons were preached by the Rev John Rattenbury, the Rev Dr Newton, and the Rev James Everett.

Inside the Methodist chapel about 1930. Soprano and tenor sat on left of the pulpit, contralto and bass on right. The harmonium behind the pulpit was hand pumped. The chapel was lit by oil lamps. FBAN.

In 1874 the chapel underwent a thorough painting and renovation, the expenses being defrayed by means of a bazaar held under the supervision of Mrs Lever, Miss Glover, Mrs Whittle, and Mrs Furmidge.

The centenary in 1929 was held first in the afternoon, with a good congregation to welcome the preacher, the Rev Benson Perkins of Birmingham. Three of the oldest members - Mrs Fairbrother, Mrs Furmidge, and Mrs G. Mabbott - helped with the tea which followed. In the evening, Mr Perkins gave an excellent lecture on "The Message of Modern Methodism". The collectors of the offertory were members of the fourth generation of Methodist families: Miss Barbara Stead, Miss Freda Fairbrother, and Miss Ena Kemp, while Miss Eva Mabbott, the other collector, represented the fifth generation.

In 1926 a new organ was installed, most of the necessary money having been raised during the previous two years. A two-manual pipe organ, it cost, with installation, £210, and was built by Messrs E Wragg & Son of Nottingham. At the afternoon service, following a dedicatory prayer, the organ was unlocked by Mrs Furnival, wife of the Rector, who also attended the opening ceremony. The organist for the occasion was Mr C Doncaster of Bingham, to whom the Committee had entrusted the choosing of the instrument.

The school room in the chapel set for a wedding reception The daffodils show that it is spring. The fedora hat on the back wall suggests a date of 1920s to 1930s. BTOW.

Harby: Village life in the Vale of Belvoir

Harby life

The public tea which followed was generously provided by friends, and the ladies presiding were Mesdames Fairbrother, Stead, T Stokes, W Kemp, R Stokes, G Mabbott, J W Bilby, W Oxbrough, Watson, and H Moulds; and Misses R Oxbrough and E Kemp. In the evening the chapel was again crowded to hear Mr Doncaster give a recital on the new organ. The Rev Warwick Armstrong gave a very interesting and amusing lecture entitled "The Lighter Side of a Parson's Life".

Inside the Methodist chapel at the Harvest Festival in 1970. The organ is in the far corner. Barbara Stead regularly played for the services. For the Communion Services people knelt on the blue carpet around the rail at the front. FBAN.

On the following Sunday afternoon a musical service was held, with solos by Mrs Stead and Mr Hemstock, the latter singing "O Rest in the Lord" in remembrance of the late Queen Alexandra. The anthems "The Lord is my Light" and "Lift up your Heads" were well rendered by the choir. Mr White of Cotgrave played the organ at both afternoon and evening services. They were well attended, and this event is still remembered in Harby.

James Wright aged 82 in 1957. He had been a Sunday School teacher at the Methodist chapel for 50 years. From the Leicester Advertiser, Saturday, October 12 1957 page 12.

A churchman once asked Dr Ford, the 18th/19th century Vicar of Melton Mowbray Parish Church, whether he was doing right, as he had pangs of conscience about his desire to leave the Anglican Church and join the Methodists. The Doctor replied in his characteristic forthright manner, "The Church, what do you call the Church? It is a number of faithful people met together to worship God, whether on a mountain, by the seaside, or wherever congregated together."

6. HARBY WOMENS INSTITUTE

HISTORY OF HARBY WOMENS INSTITUTE

'HOME AND COUNTRY'
Harby Women's Institute from "Minutes in Time" pages 1 – 2 and 4.

As a non-political, non-sectarian movement the formation of a Women's Institute provided a unique opportunity for all the women of the village to meet together as one group. One of the great motivating factors behind the WI movement was to increase food production and improve the preservation skills of home produced fruit and vegetables in the aftermath of the Great War. It also aimed to teach skills which would enable members to improve their homes and the diet, health and well-being of themselves and their families, faithfully putting into action the WI motto 'For Home and Country'. The WI encouraged thrift, commonsense, fun and companionship. Therefore the content of the monthly meetings was hopefully unlikely to inspire unseemly ambition in the women attending them or the disapproval of their menfolk or other village organizations.

In the earlier years of the WI in Harby the members do not seem to have been tempted away from the benefits of the accepted role of most women at that time - marriage. In a debate held in 1935 on the "married life versus the single life", we learn that "the single ladies made a very brave struggle for their side but the married ones gained the vote". Of course the proportion of married to single members may have had a bearing on the result!

Members showed a preference for lectures of a practical and useful nature. "How to make cuddly dolls" was not deemed one of these. Its unpopularity was such that not only was it minuted in the monthly record but also gets a special and rather sad mention in the annual report. "None of us seemed to take up making dolls, but that maybe because some of us have no little girls for whom to make them".

The Harby Women's Institute Annual General Meeting in the village hall about 1960. Mrs Herbert Watson the president is in the foreground. The lady on the right turning her head is Miss Hallam. DBUT.

Harby life

There is ample evidence to show that men were included in many WI activities. For instance at one marathon meeting in 1930 there was a cookery demonstration at 5-00 p.m. of "sea pie, scones, shortbread and roly-poly pudding", a business meeting at 6-45 p.m. followed by a gardening lecture at about 7-00 p.m., to which the men were invited. It was entitled "Dig Deep, Dig Early" and mainly concerned manures from different sources, their chemical elements and benefits. At the end of the lecture the committee served one and all with refreshments. Then came the entertainment, "The Princess of Panora" performed by Miss Reid's dramatic party. The meeting ended at 10-00 p.m.

Whist drives were a popular way to end meetings and "the men" were often allowed to come - for a small charge. At a whist drive in 1929 two sandwiches, two cakes and tea or coffee cost 3d (1 ¼ p today!). Socials took place after some meetings, or if a speaker was unable to come, as well as whole evenings devoted to raising funds for charities or special projects and these were open to the village in general. In September 1931 "after the business part of the meeting, it was thrown open to the villagers for a social evening and a very happy evening was spent. Miss Atkinson of Long Clawson gave some lovely pieces, Mr. Towler sang several songs and members of the WI held a fancy dress parade". During the evening an ankle competition took place, in the married category Mrs. W. Brown took first place and of the single ladies Miss D. Moulds was the winner. These socials served not only as a useful source of income for WI funds from the 3d entrance fee and sale of refreshments but also provided an audience for the choir, drama group and other talented members who performed at these functions.

Garden Party on the Rectory lawn on 19 July 1962, probably the WI . From left to right, back row Jack butcher, unidentified, Rev Holden, extreme right Mrs Lamin; front row third from left Dora Butcher. DBUT.

Harby life

Harby Women's Institute on an outing to Great Yarmouth. From left to right, four ladies they made friends with on the holiday, fifth Dora Butcher, Avis Wright, Sylvia Wright. The clothes suggest about 1955. DBUT.

Meetings took place in the building at the end of what is now School Lane which was called the (Men's) Institute, later the Village Institute and now the Village Hall. The running of the Institute was, it seems, definitely a male preserve, a fact to be reckoned with. For many years the WI members each paid an annual 6d subscription to the Men's Institute in order to meet there. One committee meeting 'ended abruptly' as it was time for the men to come in! For special events or extra meetings the WI would sometimes request a 'ladies night'.

Permission was needed to hold classes in the Institute room. The men raised no objection to cookery classes but dressmaking was not allowed and had to be held in the dairy mess room. Lectures at WI often created the desire to learn more and classes might be set up after a particularly interesting or useful talk.

The Women's Institute 21st birthday celebrations in the village hall, 22 October 1948. Left to right back row - Mrs Newton, Mrs Wright, Mrs Leon, Mrs Flo Oxbrough, Mrs Harriman, Mrs Brown, Mrs Nell Scarborough, Mrs Elsie Blundy, Mrs Moulds. Front row – Mrs Dickman, Enid Pick, Mrs Furmidge, Mrs Watson (President), Eva Gregory, Mrs Fairbrother. JBLU.

Harby: Village life in the Vale of Belvoir

Harby life

HARBY WI NOVEMBER MEETING *Molly Whittaker*

Molly Whittaker's poems often picked up the personalities of village individuals. Here the poem refers to the attachment of Mrs Pick to her son Harry and Mrs Dewey to the "Precious lamb" her husband. The Rector and his wife were newly arrived; Mrs Watson was President for 40 years.

Our Monthly Meeting is tonight,
We're having an election fight,
It's to elect a new committee,
To change it rather seems a pity.

After we've voted we stand and then
We all will sing "Jerusalem",
With Mrs Watson in the chair.
The business starts, there's quite a stir.

The minutes are read by our oldest member,
She loves the meeting in November,
She says, "It's such a change from jam
To get a bit of tasty spam".

And as we all are nicely sitting,
And Mrs Brown gets out her knitting,
Mrs Furmidge the accounts will read,
She's made more money than we need.

Our Christmas Party we then discuss,
This interests every one of us,
We arrange our Artists and our food,
This leaves us in a happy mood.

Now to the tables we all get,
By the committee so nicely set,
Here's Mrs Oxbrough with the pot,
We hope the tea is nice and hot.

And as we all enjoy the meal,
The village news we do reveal,
About who dies and who's to marry,
And Mrs Pick tells about "our Harry".

Miss Buxton causes lots of fun,
She'll tell your fortunes one by one,
She will show you (that is if she dares)
The winter woollies that she wears.

Our Rector's wife is rather nice,
She's only been here once or twice,
We hope she'll like us one and all,
Perhaps some day she'll on us call.

Our Nurse is there in case we're sick,
If our spam we've eaten too quick,
She's brought along her knife and fork,
She'll tell us stories of the stork.

Here's Mrs Scarborough with more tea,
She's just as busy as a bee,
And Mrs Beecham says, "Oh dear,
If only you could make it beer"

Miss Hallam from the grocery store,
Says, "I'd love a little more"
And Mrs White who's just drunk up,
Says, "It is a lovely cup".

The new committee is now read,
We hope that no one tears will shed,
We wish them all the best of luck,
And hope they'll like the washing up.

Perhaps Mrs Watson will resent,
Because she's once more President,
But a better one could not be found,
Not if we searched for miles around.

Now Mrs Dewey says, "I'll go,
My precious lamb will miss me so",
So off she goes with Mrs Clark,
Who hates to be out in the dark.

So with "The King" our meeting ends,
We say goodnight to all our friends,
"And don't forget," says Mrs Wright,
"Next month will be our party night".

Harby life

7. THE READING ROOM/VILLAGE HALL AND VILLAGE MAGAZINES

HARBY REMEMBERED..... 'THE READING ROOM'

From the Vale of Belvoir Churches Magazine, Towers and Spires, February 1996, page 29.

The Reading Room was situated on the corner of Nether Street and Langar Lane and facing the village smithy at the lower end of School Lane. It occupied the first storey above the coach house and saddle room of one of the village carriers, Samuel Starbuck. The room was a meeting place for Harby villagers where they enjoyed magic lanterns, lectures, dances and parties.

On Sunday afternoons a visiting preacher, Mr Bobby Parkes of Stathern, met with a male audience, mostly railway men, for bible studies. Mrs J Butcher, one of our oldest residents, informs me that fund raising for good causes and eventually for the proposed Institute was the province of the ladies who met on specific afternoons. Fund-raising was a tea party when brown and white bread and butter and plain cake was provided at 6d per head (2 ½ p). The saddle room was later converted into a butcher's shop, all white tiles and benches and white tiled display counter. A butcher's shop always had its own abattoir and a new building for this was erected across the paddock where the present workshop of Harby garage is sited, on the furthest corner. The Reading Room was still in use in 1919 until 1925; by then it had been felt that a village hall was needed and fund-raising had began. An area of land was donated by Mr H Furmidge nearest the Leas allotments in School Lane. The building was from an old army hut! It was widely used by workers from Eastwell Iron Ore Co, Stanton Ironworks Co., Scalford Brickyard; also Signalmen, platelayers and porters from Harby and Stathern Station (LNER and LMS). The employees of the local farms and dairy workers of the Wilts. United Dairy in the centre of the village (Watsons Lane) and Harby Farmer's Dairy Ltd (on Langar Lane) made good use of the hall.

The Reading Room is now long gone - but maybe this short article has stimulated memories of this much used facility!

School pantomime in the village hall in 1949. From left to right the children are Wendy Coy, Christine Moulds, Valerie Chambers, Thelma Rawlings, Neil Cunnington and Colin Slater. NCUN.

LATER HISTORY OF THE INSTITUTE *Leslie Cram*

The Institute in the reused army hut opened on 19 September 1925 and photographs exist showing it with its corrugated iron walls continuing little changed until the early 1950s. Then we have the invoice sent to the Secretary of the Harby Institute which reads –

"Shelbourn Son and Litchfield, Architects & Surveyors. Harby Institute. 1951 June. To professional fees for taking particulars on site and preparing plans for proposed alterations, submitting plans to Town Planning and Local Authorities and obtaining consents. Applying for Building licence. £6-6-0d."

The Harby Beacon issue of October 1952 tells us –

"It was reported at the last meeting that the contractor had promised to complete the proposed enlargement of the Institute during the winter. It was emphasised that there would be no interference with any activities which might be arranged."

Finally there is the invoice from Dan Coy, Builder, Plumber and Decorator, dated March 1953.

"To dismantling old kitchen, rebuilding new brick kitchen and boiler house as per approved plan. Removing boiler into new house. Supplying and fixing sink. Laying drain from sink to existing drain on roadside. Refixing flushing cistern and pipes to same in ladies toilet. Lining kitchen ceiling with asbestos. Plastering old brick walls. Distempering same and painting woodwork. Concreting floors and path.

£216 – 17 - 6d"

The building was always called the institute up to this time. The name is said to have changed to village hall with the numbers of new people coming to live in the village who preferred this name.

Playing cards in the Men's Institute, in the late 1940's. From the left - Jess Oxbrough, Jim Moulds (hidden), Arthur Hourd standing & Jack Butcher. JBLU.

Harby life

In the village h all about 1950. Left to right May Towers, Pidge Newton, Hilda Furmidge. Handbags and permed hair are the fashion. BTOW.

At the entrance to the village hall, Janet Wright's wedding reception, 14 April 1941, left to right - Avis Wright, Janet Wright, John Payne, Peggy Shipman. JWAT.

Wedding reception in the village hall about 1950, unidentified bride and groom with their cake at the back. On the left are Les and Peggy Shipman, Nancy and Norman Kemp. Photograph by George Skyrme, Melton Mowbray. JWAT.

VILLAGE MAGAZINES *Leslie Cram*

Serving the whole community similar to the village hall, a village magazine began in January 1951. This was the Harby Beacon, a monthly magazine costing 3d, and offering a combination of church, chapel and general village news. It ceased in January 1953. A new initiative produced the Harby News, starting in September 1970, issued quarterly at 6d a copy, and carrying a mix of events, nature and history notes and quizzes. Its editorial committee was John Bradwell, Jack Butcher, Shirley Cains, Frank Cluro, Mary Cram, Peter Furse, Richard Harrison, Ieuan Powell-Hughes, Paul Roebuck and Tom Sadler. A complete set of the Harby News is in the Record Office for Leicestershire, Leicester and Rutland.

8. PUBLIC HOUSES

HISTORY *Leslie Cram*

150 years ago there were three public houses in the village. The oldest with its timber frame is the Nag's Head. Both it and the White Hart are shown on the 1790 map as is the third pub, the Marquis of Granby situated in what is now two houses made from the original one where Boyers Orchard meets Stathern Road. They are all listed in the earliest trade directory in 1846, George Hallett, victualler of the Marquis of Granby, John Haywood, victualler of the White Hart and John Whittle, victualler of the Nag's Head. The Marquis of Granby is last mentioned in the 1871 census; after this only the Nag's Head and White Hart are recorded.

The back garden of 42 Stathern Lane. This was once the Marquis of Granby Inn. The Inn had closed by 1875 and the building was made into two cottages. NCUN.

Harby life

Looking south along Main Street about 1910. The White Hart is on the right and the chapel school room on the left. Above the door to the White Hart is written "Bertie Cox". HCOY.

In the White Hart about 1950, from left to right Jim Banner, Ellis White, Stan Wilcox, Molly Whittaker, Geoff Furmidge, Les (Pudding) Whittaker, Noel Furmidge. DWHI.

The White Hart about 1947. The children are Neil Cunnington and Iris Slater. A postcard by Landscape View M Harborough. JWAT.

148   Harby: Village life in the Vale of Belvoir

Harby life

In the Nag's Head about 1950. From left to right Derek Brown, Jim Towers, Roy Brown, unidentified, Don Whittaker, Stodge Manchester. Ken Cresswell has the back of his head to us in the foreground. BTOW.

The Nag's Head about 1965 with the new bus shelter. CBOO.

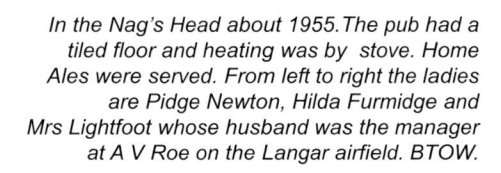

In the Nag's Head about 1955. The pub had a tiled floor and heating was by stove. Home Ales were served. From left to right the ladies are Pidge Newton, Hilda Furmidge and Mrs Lightfoot whose husband was the manager at A V Roe on the Langar airfield. BTOW.

Harby: Village life in the Vale of Belvoir

Harby life
9. SCOUTS AND GUIDES

HISTORY *Leslie Cram*

To run a Scout or Guide troop in the Harby area has usually meant drawing boys and girls from more than one village. And there are not all that many people willing and able to run a troop. So Scout and Guide troops in the village have been formed and disbanded as there have been keen adults wishing to lead and children keen to join. We were off to a good start with Fred Pepper, who kept the Post Office and village store, who was warranted as Scoutmaster to the Harby Troop in 1911 only three years after the movement began with Baden-Powell's "Scouting for Boys" published in 1908. The Scouts in Melton Mowbray began the year before. Baden-Powell himself knew our area as he was a friend of the Duke of Rutland at the time and visited the Castle.

There are no records after that apart from a couple of photographs of Harby girls as Guides at camp away from the village. They may have belonged to a troop based in a nearby village.

Don Whittaker in his Boy Scout uniform aged about 12 in 1944. Taken in their studio by Heawood & Son, Melton Mowbray. DWHI.

The Scout troop which started in 1943 was the First Harby and Stathern, run by the station master and connected with the United States airforce personnel at Langar airfield at that time. The US airforce moved out in 1944 but for a while kept in touch with Harby Scouts by letter. When the Canadian airforce moved into Langar in 1952 they initiated a Scout Troop, this time meeting in Langar. Harby boys went there and it continued after the Canadians left in 1963.

Harby life

Shortly after arriving in Harby in 1951, John and Anne Dames were asked by the Rev Holden if they would be able to set up a Scout Troop and a Girl Guide Company. Both had been in the Guide and Scout movements for a long time.

The Scout Troop first met in a room in the Rectory, then the Village Hall. Members were always on the low side, normally ten to twelve boys with John Dames as Scout master. Help was given for a short while by Mr Wilf Darby. The various scouting activities, such as learning the Scout Laws, tying knots, tracking, fire lighting and cooking were undertaken and map and compass reading practised. Church services such as St. George's Day and Armistice Day were attended. As the local boys moved into work and Mr Dames's part time teaching at Evening Institutes increased together with family duties, numbers declined and the Scout Troop was brought to an end around 1953.

The 1st Harby Guide Company was formed in 1951 and approximately 12 girls from the village joined with Anne Dames the Leader. Meetings were held in the Village Hall. During the next two years a Guide Company from Nottingham visited Harby and were taken round the village and for walks along the canal. A visit was made to Nottingham Council House in Old Market Square and Harby Guides were given a conducted tour. A weekend camp was held at Knipton during the summer months.

In the early 1970s girls from Harby went to Scalford for their nearest Company until Valerie Skelton and Pat Barrett re-established the First Harby Girl Guides.

Harby Girl Guides camping near Knipton about 1951. From left to right they are Iris Brown, Betty Haynes, Pearl Rawlings, possibly Cherry Walker, Sylvia Wright and Ann Hillsdon. ADAM.

Harby life
MY FIRST CAMP
Nicola Biggadike, from Harby News 1971 issue 5 page 2.

This summer I became a Guide in the 1st Scalford and Eastwell Company. On Wednesday morning, 3rd August, I went with Karen Palmer, Yvonne Coy, Sarah Blundy, and Jill Swingler to wait at the Barton's Bus Depot for the coach that was taking us to Dethick, near Matlock, for our Guide Camp.

When we got to Dethick, we unloaded all of our things from the coach, and pitched one of the tents before we had our lunch. Afterwards we pitched the rest of the tents, and everyone was given a special job to do. Mine was to collect wood for making a fire to cook on.

Whilst we were at camp we had a few outings. We went to Matlock to see the Venetian Nights and Illuminations, and also to see the Abraham Heights with the Rutland Cavern. At Matlock Bath we went swimming. Another day we went to Riber Castle and Zoo.

The thing I remember most about camp was the midnight feast. We all went to bed at the usual time, and Susan set her alarm clock which she had brought from home. The alarm went off at exactly twelve o'clock. It made us all jump. We heard many footsteps, and other Guides from other tents came to join us. Everyone brought something. We had cyd-apple pop, shandy, and lemonade to drink. We had already used our mugs for soup, and had not washed them, but no-one minded very much. To eat, we had biscuits, sweets, and chocolate. We did not clean our teeth because it was too dark, and there were no mothers about. Sarah Blundy missed the whole feast because she didn't wake up.

Another thing I shall remember was the bad storm we had the night before we came home. We went to bed at about a quarter-to-nine. At nine o'clock we had to get up and put our macs on. Then we had to pack our bedding into plastic bags, and take everything over to a big farm barn. There was a big storm going on with lots of thunder and lightning. In the barn there were many other Guides from another Company. We were all packed into two small rooms. We did not mind the storm at all, but we didn't like all the mouse-holes in the barn.

The next day we dried the tents and took them down to pack them. Then we took all the luggage and tents down to the farmyard, where the coach met us. Some Guides helped the driver to pack the coach, and the rest of us went to search for litter. We then collected the rest of our belongings and got into the coach, and set off for home.

That is how my first camp ended, and I hope that next year I can go again.

10. SPORT

HARBY CRICKET CLUB *Rex Stapleford*

The earliest record of playing of cricket in our area is the match played in 1858 at Eastwell between 22 members of the Eastwell Yeomen's Club and an All England Eleven. First class cricket was not played by Leicestershire County Cricket Club until 1894. But a Melton League was in existence in the 1890s when Harby is mentioned for the first time. In 1897 the championship was decided between Harby and Waltham, the match being played at Harby. Harby scored 58 against Waltham's total of 42. The Harby players in this game were J M Goodson, J J Jackson, R Furmidge, J Hassall, A M Smith, R Rowbottom, H Furmidge, junior, J W Haywood, C Martin, W Furmidge, junior, and G Barke. The top scorer for Harby was C Martin with 16 runs and the best bowling performance for Harby was J Haywood with 5 for 12.

The earliest evidence within the village for a cricket club is a photograph dating around 1900. The surviving minutes start in 1919 when the club met for the first time after the First World War, having closed down during the war. In 1921 the minutes record the resignation of the secretary after 30 years' service so we can definitely date the village team as existing in 1891 and with the example of Eastwell, it possibly existed twenty years before.

Cricket team on the playing field to west of the church about 1900. Sitting on ground fourth from left is Sam Furmidge. Behind the man sitting with the cricket bat is Mr Edwards holding something in his left had. POBR.

Harby life

Up until 1938, the ground was let free to the club by Harry Furmidge of the adjacent Hall Farm. This arrangement was probably instigated by his father, William Hardy Furmidge. After this date the club was charged a nominal fee for the hire of the field. There was a pavilion, as the minutes record in 1924. In 1920 it had been decided to fence the ground full length and about 15 yards wide.

As well as friendly matches arranged with other villages Harby took part in matches played to raise funds for charity: the Hospital Cup and the Nursing Cup. The village also played in three leagues:- Hickling, the Vale of Belvoir and Melton and District. At the 1922 AGM it was stated that the Hickling League Secretary would arrange the league fixtures. The League comprised Harby, Hickling, Upper Broughton, Nether Broughton, Kinoulton, Hose, and Long Clawson. Hickling Cricket Club put up a cup for competition. The Rev Canon Ashmell, the vicar of Hickling, stated that he would present a bat for the best batting average, and a pair of leg guards for the best bowling average.

Harby cricket team about 1950 in front of the Harby pavilion. From left to right - Back row - Jim Rawlings, Noel Furmidge, Bill Newton, Bernard Haywood, Charlie Hourd, unknown. Front row - Walter Pick, Claude Rawlings, Ernie Towers, Sam Furmidge, Mr Cook from Barkstone, Mack Hoyes. BTOW.

The Vale of Belvoir League was first formed in 1923, and was effectively the re-named Hickling and District League. As well as Harby, the teams involved in this league were Stathern, Old Dalby, Long Clawson, Hose, Hickling and Nether Broughton. Harby also played in the Melton and District League which was re-formed in 1932.

Harby cricket team 1959 Belvoir League runners-up at Ab Kettleby. From left to right - back row: Peter Hubbard, Ben Walker, Peter Stapleford, Derek Ward, Jack Clarke. Front row: Colin Moulds, Ian Slater, Charlie Musson, John Walker, Jim Towers, Sam Towers. BTOW.

Between the First and Second World Wars it was a tradition to have a cricket fixture during "Harby Feast" week. This was sometimes a team from Nottingham, organised by Hardy Furmidge, senior, Harry Furmidge's brother, who was the head groundsman at W Foremans in Nottingham. During the afternoon of the Saturday of the 1936 'Feast Week' a match was played between a Belvoir Estates team, and Hardy Furmidge's team which included several Notts. County Cricket Club players. Among these were Staples, Lilley and Iremonger. As reported in the Grantham Journal, the vagaries of the ground did not allow high scores, and Hardy's team won by 91 to 79. Albert Iremonger scored 52 for the winners, and C Lowater was 24 not out for the losers.

The wicket was not used for the six years of the Second World War, 1939-1945. At the first postwar meeting in 1946 a committee was formed to inspect the pitch and pavilion: Sam Furmidge, Jim Moulds, Jack Clarke, Leslie Whittaker, Cyril Hilsdon and Frank Wright. As it turned out only Sam Furmidge and Jim Moulds braved the elements for the inspection. However Mr Newton, representing Messrs Roberts of Bottesford, came along and it was determined that none of the old fencing or wire was of any further use, and Mr Newton said he would let the Hon. Secretary have a tender for the job. Mr Newton added his willingness to carry out the pavilion repairs himself. At a meeting in October 1946, arrangements were made for attending to the ground and Jack Bilby was asked to turf the pitch. At the AGM of 1947 it was agreed to approach Messrs

Harby life

Gunn & Moore of Nottingham, to specify marl to treat a pitch 30 yards by 20 yards. In the last decade of the club a second pavilion was purchased from Plungar Cricket Club, after their club had ceased to exist and re-erected at Harby at the side of the existing pavilion.

After the Second World War in addition to the Hospital Cup and the Nursing Cup, Harby competed in the Salaman Cup, St Dunstans Cup, British Legion Cup, Charity Cup and the Quarries Cup.

Sadly, in 1964, because of lack of interest, it was decided at a meeting held at the Nag's Head, that the cricket club could not carry on. However, it can be said that club had lots of success in its estimated 100 year history.

Within the limitations of the available information, the following summarises the club's successes from 1919:

Hickling and District League: 1925 runners-up.
Belvoir League: Champions 1949, 1958, 1961, joint runners-up 1925, 1929, 1948 and 1959.
Melton League: Champions 1935, 1936, 1937, (1939?), 1948, 1949, 1951 (joint), runners-up 1952
Nursing Cup: Champions 1935, 1939, 1950, losing finalists 1951 (actually played in 1952), 1954 and 1957.
Hospital Cup: Champions 1937, 1947, losing finalists 1948 and 1951.
St Dunstan's Cup: Losing Finalists 1947. They were also finalists in 1957 v Scalford (no record of result).
Katz Junior Cup: Losing finalists 1949.

Further details of players and scores are to be found in Rex Stapleford's book, "A history of Harby cricket club 1919 to 1964."

Cricket match on the playing field west of the church around 1950. On the horizon is Hall Farm and the trees round the church are on the left. The parked cars by the farm give an indication of date. BCLA.

Harby life

CRICKET IN THE RAIN *From an undated newspaper account*

Played on in Raincoats!

There are those who maintain that bad sportsmanship is on the increase. It is refreshing therefore to record the following incident which took place at a cricket match in the Melton and District League recently. The match was between Plungar and Harby and the Plungar team was dismissed for a small score.

While Harby were batting rain tumbled down, and there was every justification for the players to abandon the game. Harby were in a winning position, but the Plungar men, instead of appealing against continuance of play, went to the Pavilion for their raincoats and played until Harby had scored the winning hit.

FOOTBALL *Leslie Cram*

Football was for the winter months. There were two pitches where the village played, one along Stathern Lane, the other belonging to Ellis White down Colston Lane. There were keen supporters and Molly Whittaker wrote this poem about the team around 1950.

Harby United football team 1947-48 season. From left to right—back row - R (Cracker) Musson, Geoff (Peg) Furmidge, E (Ted) Alderman, Dennis (Hourdy) Hourd, Brian (Farmer) Wilford, J (Bufton) Wilford (captain). Front - E (Ernest) Manchester, T (Tommy) Jackson, Jack (Trigger) Smith, F (Frank) Robinson, H (Harry) Eatherington. The boy at the front with the ball is Michael Richmond, son of the Trainer Alf Richmond, thought to have had the nick name "Goballs". BTOW.

Harby: Village life in the Vale of Belvoir

Harby life

Harby and Stathern United football team at the football pitch in Ellis White's field along Colston Lane in the mid 1940s against a German PoW team from the Redmile camp. Left to Right - Back row Albert Marsden, Cracker Musson, Tommy Jackson, Brian Wilford, Ted Alderman, Stan Moulds, John Wilford, Jack Pepper, Alf Richmond. Front Row - Bunny Pizer, Harry Shipman, Les Shipman, Mick O'Leary, Harry Scarborough. We are indebted to Harry Shipman of Stathern for the identification of the players and the occasion. DWHI.

HARBY FOOTBALL CLUB *Molly Whittaker*

At Harby we have a football team
Of which we are very proud
And if a home match they should play
You ought to see the crowd.

The goalie is a chap named Ted
His saves are really swell.
He saves what looks like certain goals
And penalties as well.

The left full back is 'Bufton',
He is a great attacker,
The chap who plays at right full back
Is known to all as 'Cracker'.

At centre half is 'Hourdy'
Who shows amazing skill.
To watch his perfect ball control
It gives the crowd a thrill.

A chap called 'Peg' is right half,
He clears the ball quite well.
He fouls the opponent's forwards
But the goals he scores are swell.

'Farmer Brian' is the left half
His play is neat and clean.
His passes to the centre
Are as good as any seen.

On the right wing we have 'Ernest'
Who's as swift as any hare.
The inside right we know as 'Frank'
He does quite good work there.

Our centre forward's super
He's full of vim and vigour,
He heads and shoots some smashing goals,
He's known to all as 'Trigger'.

Now 'Tommy' is the inside left
He shoots so straight and true.
The outside left is 'Harry'
He is so tricky too.

Mr Scarborough, he's the linesman,
Who waves a little flag.
Mr Richmond he's the trainer
And has a little 'Bag'.

The person at the matches
Who the players like to see
Is Mrs Brown who at half time
Brings them all some tea.

The secretary he is 'Albert'
Who works hard for the team.
He arranges all the matches
As a sports man he's quite keen.

So here's to the United
We hope a cup they'll win
Then we'll take it to the local
And fill it full of gin.

Harby life

Boys of Harby Football Team
We should like you all to know
How very proud we are of you
And our gratitude to show.

It is a great achievement
That you two cups should win
You've always tried to play the game
Ere you should lose or win.

You all served in the forces
When duty called you all
And this makes us feel extra proud
When we see you play football.

A special word for Captain John
Whose heart is in the game,
His example to his team mates
Has helped his team to fame.

To the Secretary and Committee
We also say thank you
For a Saturday afternoon of sport
The football season through.

And now the season's over
And you boys the cups have won
From spectators who support the team
We say 'Good Lads, Well Done!'.

Football match about 1950 in Ellis White's field near the mill on Colston Lane. Sherbrooke House can be seen to the left of the goal posts. BCLA.

Harby life

FOX HUNTING

Belvoir Hunt in the field to south west of church in the 1960s. JWAT.

GONE TO EARTH *Betty Holyland*

A good day's hunting now was done,
In yellow mist the sun was lost,
Like trimmings on a Christmas cake,
Each hedgerow leaf was edged in frost.

Horses and hounds were boxed at last,
It had not been their day.
Old "Reynard" had them all "out-foxed"
As in the ditch nearby he lay.

Silent and low - just waiting there,
Hidden in dappled light - quite still.
Waiting 'til all was clear at last,
To hug the hedge up Harby hill.

The tawny shadow held his stride,
Listening for the sound of men.
Then never halting in his pace,
Made straight the line for earth and den.

The ancient spring has slaked his thirst,
Lifting his mask to scan the Vale,
Knowing that now all chase is past,
He "fox-trots" home as daylight pales.

Harby life

SKATING *Leslie Cram*

Older inhabitants of the village commonly remember the winters being colder than in recent years with the canal frozen over for weeks or months at a time. Photos back to 1894 show villagers out on the ice. Sometimes people are wearing skates and Freda Fairbrother remembers people who could skate to the Trent and back in a day.

Skating on the canal near Langar Bridge in 1946. The bridge is on the left. BCLA

TENNIS *Leslie Cram*

The Rectory was the biggest house with the largest gardens in the village. It often served to provide for the church and social activities. One of these was tennis, with numerous photos from the 1920s. The court was grass with the lines laid out in white and metal netting to keep the balls in the playing area. Girls are shown in the dresses of the time to just below the knee, sometimes in special white tennis dresses with white plimsolls and Sunday best hats.

Old Rectory tennis court about 1925. The girls have all special tennis shoes and tunics. They are wearing their best cloche hats in the fashion of the time. CBOO.

11. EXCURSIONS

DAY TRIPS AND EXCURSIONS
Harby Women's Institute from "Minutes in Time" page 85.

Day trips featured regularly in WI activities. Pre-war, the June meeting was set aside for outings, often to a seaside resort like Skegness or Hunstanton. After visiting Chatsworth in 1929, "members came home wiser and better women"! Members saved up monthly in a "holiday club" to pay for the big day out. Another popular option was Sandringham but in 1937 a break with tradition saw them off to Liverpool and Port Sunlight, "a happy day was spent by all, not a hitch happened until coming home, poor Mrs. Buxton got something in her eye but was attended to at Boots in Nottingham".

They stayed closer to home in 1933 and 34 visiting the Be-Ro and Players factories in Nottingham. Following the flour factory tour the ladies were entertained to tea with "several going to the pictures" afterwards. The fifty who went round Players finished up. . . ., where? The next page is missing!

In 1933 the "summer outing was not a success", we do not know why but this was rare. In contrast, 1948 saw them venture to Windsor, visiting the castle as well as taking "a river trip of 22 miles through the beautiful wooded country of Marlow. This was one of the best outings we have ever had." They pledged to return at some future date.

From the 1950s evening outings tended to replace the full day ones. The "mystery trips" are fondly recalled. The popularity of outings began to dwindle as more members began to work outside the home and membership numbers dropped. The times when daughters of members joined up as teenagers and stayed in the village were passing. Filling a bus when membership is over 100 is much easier than when it is well under fifty. The job of outings organiser needs someone of exceptional ability and unfailing enthusiasm in order to make a success of it.

Trips to potteries, museums and gardens happened regularly. It became more of a struggle to fill the bus and as coach hire charges became higher, inevitably, financial losses were a growing risk. A clear lack of viability has ended, at least temporarily, regular outings. We confine ourselves to local venues, or have a walk followed by supper.

Skegness 13 July 1931 photographed by Walking Pictures. Left to right Jim Towers, Flo Oxbrough, May Towers, Madge Brown with her son Derek in the pram. The children have buckets and spades ready for the beach. The ladies are wearing the latest fashions with cloche hats, shoes with heels and strap, and calf length coats with no belt. BTOW.

Harby life

Coach outing about 1956 possibly to Blackpool. The people are:-

1 Unknown
2 Bernard Haywood
3 Unknown
4 Unknown
5 Janet Dewey
6 Claude Hourd
7 Ben Dewey
8 Steve Wass
9 Unknown
10 Julia Brown
11 Bernard Clark
12 Mrs Wass
13 Dora Butcher
14 Possibly Roy Brown
15 Unknown
16 Unknown
17 Frank Moulds
18 Charley Pym
19 May Brown
20 Joyce Pym(nee Brown)
21 Jimmy Towers
22 Possibly Derek Ward
23 May Towers
24 Derek Brown
25 Ralph Moulds
26 Hilda Furmidge (nee Moulds)

DBUT.

Coach excursion about 1940. Back row second from left Rose Moulds, next to her is Dick Tinsley, then Ralph Moulds the driver with his hair elegantly parted down the middle. In the middle row, second from left is May Towers then Pidge Newton. From left to right on the front row seventh Don Whittaker, the boy with the stick Ron Lamin, Denis Hourd holding John Hourd his little brother standing with blond hair. BTOW.

Harby: Village life in the Vale of Belvoir

12. CELEBRATIONS

THE HORTICULTURAL SHOW
Harby Women's Institute from "Minutes in Time" pages 76 – 80.

In 1891 the schedule for the show, run by Harby Horticultural Society, listed, amongst the usual fruit, flowers and vegetables of more modern shows, classes for farm produce. Barley, oats, wheat, turnips and mangolds were to be contested but surely the hottest competition was for the cheese class. Many of the village farmhouses had dairies, like Starbuck House, and made their own Stilton cheese. A poultry section of several classes was also included. Music was provided by a band and choir, with races, a tug-o-war and a bicycle race to add to the entertainment.

After the formation of the WI the members soon became involved, taking charge of the show for the first time in 1928. The sporting events still included a tug-o-war and a few pert remarks were made about "the fat ones" when the team was chosen. However, after that, the only sport mentioned is the annual cricket match between Harby WI XI and a neighbouring WI or village ladies XI. In 1929 Harby beat the Hose team at cricket and "altogether it was a lovely day, the only fly in the ointment being strained muscles for the president and a sprained ankle for the secretary but no bones broken and nobody died". Undaunted they played the Harby men's XI the next year but the latter had to play "left handed and with broom sticks"!

The schedules for the show were printed and handed out in June. The 1930 schedule included extra classes for peas and lettuces. Jams from "hard and soft" fruits and marmalade, along with currant cake and plain cake and both brown and white eggs. In the flower section they agreed there should be "6 varieties of blooms". No exhibits were to be removed before 7-15 p.m. but all to be out by 8 o'clock. In 1933 they had 200 exhibits.

Who was to open the fete and judge the exhibits occupied the committee for several months before the show - some like Miss Wright opened the fete and judged the home produce section while Mr. Townsend from Melton judged the horticultural. Another time Miss Hill was to open the fete and with "her housekeeper and gardener along with Mrs. Ransome's gardener and probably Mrs. Ransome as well", judge the exhibits. On the other hand, "Mrs. Paravicini (was) to be asked to bring some of her staff for judging etc., the Misses Paravicini would supply jazz music", an added bonus.

In 1935 excuses were made for Mrs. Munro, who was supposed to open the fete, by her fellow judges. However, "Mrs. Munro did come in the evening, and gave a splendid talk on WI activities". In 1938 Miss Ellis "gave a little talk on the Spanish troubles, after tea".

This was not the end of a very busy day, for at 8 o'clock, the dance would begin in the Institute room. Admission to this was 3d in 1930, with music provided by their own Miss Buxton, so with no outgoings, the dance must have helped swell the funds - that year they made £16-10-0d on the whole day.

Harby life

The opening of the fourth annual exhibition of the Harby Horticultural Society, perhaps held at Hall Farm, see the stack in the background, on September 24 in the late 1800s. The Rector, Rev Norman, is apparently reading from the Bible. The gentlemen show a rich variety of headgear (no ladies appear in the photogaph), with a Sherlock Holmes type outfit just to the left of Rev Norman and an Italian style flat hat on the gentleman with the clerical collar second from the left. The photograph was taken by James Norman the Rector's son. BTOW.

Prizes for the winning exhibits were, it seems, given out some days later. In 1932, for instance "Mr. Dickman to be asked for use of tables and trestles and to get help to fix same. Friday night to be the evening to give prizes away at 7-00 p.m., committee ladies to take charge of the tea".

For many years Harby WI relied on the proceeds from the annual flower show and fete to finance its activities and up until the war, the July meeting was almost entirely taken up with finalising the arrangements for it. First on the agenda was the proposal that members would give food for the tea. Each year this was passed and a group set up, usually with Mrs. Dickman in charge, consisting of the committee and 10 or 12 other members. One of the group would sell the tickets, two others collect them in, the rest were to pour out or be waitresses. In 1932 they had a "plain tea consisting of white or brown bread and butter, barm loaves, plain and plum cake and victoria sandwiches". All this for 6d. In the same year Mrs. Howitt and Mrs. Herrick were engaged as "two special caretakers to see to the copper, put out and wash tea things and sweep up the Institute floor after the exhibits were removed, 2/6d paid to each". For a further 1/6d apiece, they were asked to "scrub out the kitchen and clear up the room".

Next, those in charge of the stalls and games were named. Not surprisingly these were usually the same people on the same stalls, year after year. They ran a refreshment stall and a gift stall "from which nothing must be sold before the opening." Others looked after 'the bran tub, Id in the bath, Treasure Hunt, Spots on the Umbrella' and so on. The skittles, played by the men, were looked after by helpful husbands - often Mr Dickman and Mr Towler. The prize for winning the skittles in 1932 was 5/-, whilst that for the Treasure Hunt was "according to the takings." A fortune teller was normally one of the attractions but there were sometimes problems filling the post. Mrs. West was asked to come, for a fee, one year but then could not - the next choice was found to have gone to Ireland! Who finally provided the "Peeps into the Future" at 6d a go the minutes do not say - perhaps it was Miss Buxton, who did it on another occasion.

During the afternoon an entertainment of some sort took place. For instance, an exhibition of folk dancing in 1933 for which "Mr. Kemp had been asked to fetch the piano to the field". He was presumably asked to do the same the following year when a group of schoolgirls gave a dancing display "on the grass". Another time they had a fancy dress parade open to all. "Two classes, comic and general and a class for children".

The first show during the war was held in August 1941 starting at 5-00 p.m. It appears to have been simply a produce show with about 25 classes and no stalls. These were re-introduced the following year when they had "well worth" rummage and provision stalls, together with some side shows and a mystery parcel. This show made a profit of £ 38-11-10½d, £30 of which was to be sent to "our boys in the forces", as was the bulk of the profit in 1943.

These two shows had been held on Feast Monday - the same date as all the pre-war ones. However, there is no reported return of the cricket matches or the dances in the evenings. Just "an ankle competition after tea" and "a later tea arranged for the children at a quarter to five" are mentioned. There was no return either of devoting the July meeting to the arrangements for the show, just a short extra meeting held in early September for this, with a whist drive after the business was done. The special prize giving ceremony disappeared too and awards were handed out at the next monthly meeting.

The evening dances did make a return and fond memories of the "flannel dance" remain, this was an occasion for informal dress, as opposed to the usual dressy ones. According to the show accounts, dances ceased for good after 1954. Somehow the excitement of the event, so evident in the early minutes, did not survive long after the war. Perhaps people were just older and weary from the years of worry and austerity.

The days of enthusiastic participation by members such as May Brown who, although living in only one room, managed to enter all the classes each year, were passing.

Less and less is written about the shows through the 1950s and 60s, just an addition or two to the schedule like "a window plant" and "polyanthus roses". Profits from the show peaked in 1950 with a total of £52, after that profits overall begin to fall away and in 1969 only £10 was realized. It has to be assumed that it was then decided to cease holding the show, although the minutes make no specific reference to this.

Harby life
HARBY FEAST
Nora Blaze from Harby News issue 13 pages 12 to 13.

People born in Harby do not need to be told that the annual Feast is on the Sunday after September 19th, with the Harvest Supper to follow. It passes quietly these days, but as the following extract from a press-cutting of 1870 will show, it used to be one of the highlights of the year.

"The great rejoicings which took place at our Feast were such as to call forth the general remark that nothing has been equal to it for the last half-century. From Sunday morning, the 26th, until Tuesday there was a considerable influx of respectable visitors, who vied with each other in contributing to the happiness of their fellows.

"Friend Jackson as usual supplied the finest beef for strengthening the inner man, and our two hostelries poured forth copious libations. The whole of the sports were 'pulled off' with great satisfaction and without accident, except that one or two individuals who, instead, tried the Blondinian system and came to grief. The jingling race 'Ada Elliott' was well performed amid roars of laughter, and all the running and jumping etc., was admirably got through. Out of three cricket matches, Harby were victorious in two of them. For two days all was joy, jollity and happiness, and nothing occurred to mar the enjoyment of all who had the pleasure of being present. The dance of the ladies and gentlemen upon the greensward was a pretty sight in the faint moonlight, and contributed much to the happiness of those engaged. The best thanks are due to the gentleman who kindly lent his field for the occasion, and we are sure Harby Feast of 1870 will not soon be forgotten."

HARBY FEAST AS IT USED TO BE
Edith Buxton from Harby Beacon, October 1952.

Weeks before the feast, preparations began. Excitement was rife amongst the children, for the roundabouts, stalls, swinging boats, coconut alleys and gaily painted caravans were expected. On the Thursday before the Feast they duly arrived in the public house paddock. The thrill of seeing the erection of the fair and the counting-over of coppers saved for weeks followed. Finally, on the Saturday evening, the organ blared forth "Goodbye Sally I must leave you", the rifles banged at the rifle range, the swings swung high and the coconuts were knocked off at "3 balls a penny". How we treasured our goldfish, bought for 6d. complete with glass bowl! Sunday saw both Church and Chapel full of grateful people lustily singing "Come ye thankful people come" and the collection, which was always £5 and over, was sent to Nottingham General Hospital. Then the Monday brought two shows – the Horticultural and the Poultry in Mr Furmidge's field. There was friendly rivalry over the onions and potatoes and the late Mr Dick Wilford's heavyweight marrows for which he won the late Mr C Rawlinson's prize of 2/6d. The cricket match attracted a great crowd and the proceedings were generally enlivened by the Long Clawson Band with its tunes of "Sally get out of the donkey's way" and "Knees up, Mother Brown". Tuesday evening brought Miss Starbuck's Concert in the School. Here the comedian sang annually of "the shipwrecked boat" and how he "knocked a hole in the bottom to let the water out". This concert would benefit the Belvoir Nursing Association by £6. And a word about the Feast Fare: - Roast Beef, Plum Puddings, Damson Pies, Cold Chicken, Trifles and Stilton cheese. Beer and wine flowed freely for there were many visitors to be entertained. Friends of many years met and had a chat and a drink at the good old Harby Feast. May all these good things soon return.

A FEAST OF FLOWERS
Harby Women's Institute from "Minutes in Time" page 75.

In its heyday, Harby Feast was a long weekend of celebrations when families gathered together with friends and relatives, often from far afield, to eat, drink and enjoy a multitude of entertainments. There was a constant stream of arrivals at the Harby and Stathern railway station coming to join in the fun. Feast Sunday is the first Sunday following September 19th, so it is essentially a harvest time event.

The arrival and setting up of the funfair began proceedings and on the Saturday everyone enjoyed the traditional coconut shy, rifle range, roundabouts and swings. Sunday was reserved for church or chapel harvest services. Feast Monday was the big day, centred round the horticultural and agricultural show, along with music, fun and sports of all kinds. Quantities of all manner of foods were consumed, roast beef, cold chicken, plum puddings, trifle and Stilton cheese. Frumenty, made from boiled wheat with spice and fruit was always part of the fare on offer. The Feast usually concluded with a concert. The whole village was alive with activity as the long weeks of preparation culminated in this once a year highlight.

HARBY CORONATION FIREWORK DISPLAY 1937.
From the Nottingham Guardian.

THE SMILING VALE OF BELVOIR

THE Vale of Belvoir is chuckling over the firework display that wound up the Coronation festivities at the Leicestershire village of Harby. In the presence of 150 spectators (writes a correspondent) the stewards carried a fine clothes basket of rockets and the like to the scene of operations.

Watching an attendant sorting the fireworks with a naked light, sparks dropping, one had an intuition that Harby was on the eve of a momentous display. It arrived all right. I think it was a set piece, entitled " Franco bombs Harby." A sudden flash and bang!

Rockets to right of us;
Crackers to left of us;
Onward we thundered.
Into the schoolyard we rushed;
Someone had blundered.

Harby life

Rockets chased the fleeing spectators like whippets and rattled a lively tattoo on the sides of motor cars.

Presently, all was quiet. The gently burning clothes basket lit up the wan faces of the Harbyites peeping round the walls and over the tops of hedgerows. Slowly they emerged from their shelters. The insurgents had retired. The display was over in three minutes, and Harby went to bed.

13. HOME LIFE

JOAN WATSON'S DIARY 1969

Joan Watson and her husband Robert, sometimes referred to in the diary as Robert, sometimes as Bossie, lived in Dairy House in Watson's Lane beside the dairy where Robert's parents had been managers. Robert's mother was called "The Misses" by her employees and Joan uses the term in the diary. Sis and Sally Moulds were their neighbours to whom they often went for tea on Sunday afternoons. Mr Stilton and Mr Cornell were employed at the dairy. Others mentioned are predominantly Joan's friends and relations. Joan's relatives were her sister Peg with husband Les at Sherbrooke Farm, her cousins Enid, married to Walter Pick, and Queen, and her aunt Lois. Joan's friends were Jane (Janet Dewey), Connie (Green, nee Dickman). Brenda was a haberdashery shop in Melton, and Allans were the bakers at Scalford who came round Harby selling bread from their van. Pells were butchers in Plungar. Silcocks were a local agricultural merchants. Jack B (Butcher) did many jobs for Joan and the dairy. The travelling library van came on alternate Thursdays.

The moon landing in the diary is something we all know about already. Those who were alive at the time remember what we were doing when we heard. Joan misheard the name Aldrin for the more usual Aldwin.

May Towers in her living room at Wharflands in the 1950s. As typical of the period, the room is decorated with patterns on the wall, chairs and cushions and decorative lace on the back of the chairs. BTOW.

July.

Sun 13. Breezy very warm. Real summer weather. Lovely day. Had cold lunch. Took tea up to Sis and Sallys. Enid, Walter, Queen and Mrs Warner stayed out until 9.15.

Mon 14. Hot after misty morning. Washed. Picked raspberrys for deep freeze. Pat Scarboro' called. Jack B cut my Lawn.

Tue 15. Very very warm again. Very hot afternoon. Peg went to uncle Harolds cremation at Loughboro'. Nick went Peteborough show, 90 degrees. Q and E called after W.I. at Misses.

Wed 16. Very hot and clear again. 100 degrees on wall thermometer. BLAST OFF TO MOON. ARMSTRONG, ALDWIN, COLLINS.

Thu 17. Very warm. Library. Jane called. Enid called.

Fri 18. Very warm. Robert and Mr London went to (? Hanley, Henley, Harby or Harley). Connie stayed night.

Sat 19. Very warm, slight cloud. Robert and Mr London came back 4.30. Went to Pegs at night. Peg went to hospital abcess. Cooler night.

Sun 20. Lovely day. TOUCHED DOWN MOON 9.18. Went Chadwell and Goadby church. Went Granby Flower Festival.

Mon 21. Very very warm. MAN WALKED ON MOON 3.56 am. LIFT OFF 6.54 pm. DOCKED SAFELY. Bought skirt, tops Brenda.

Tue 22. Called at Pells at night. Very very warm again. June Hemsley came, what a upshot. Michael left and Monica Irene fed baby. Went to Knipton with prizes to Lady Hill-Woods for cons.

Wed 23. Hot again. Humid, especially at night. Absolute deluge during night. Lightning but little thunder. Aunt Lo brought bible.

Thu 24. Cloudy but warm. Cleared during day. Bright evening. Bossie left for Bristol at 7 a.m. Enid came across. Bossie rang from Cirencester 6.30 to say he'd be back by 9.30 to 10. Peg been hospital with Jane. SPLASH DOWN COMPLETE. PRESIDENT ON BOARD.

Fri 25 Bossie went Egginton then on to Aston. Got home 9 o'clock. Very Warm. Charles Moulds died.

Sat 26. Washed hair. Very warm again after cloudy start. Humid. Went to Hose church fete. Libby came night.

Notes. ARMSTRONG AND ALDWIN WALKED ON MOON 21ST 3.56 am.

Harby life

Sun 27. Brighter, warm. Had tea up at Sis and Sallys. Went to Queens for supper, very nice. Milk came from Whitchurch.

Mon 28. Dreadful day. Poured with rain all day. Mr Stilton and Mr Cornell. English Country Cheese Council. Took them to Grantham. Poured. Bought 6 chairs £15.

Tue 29. Paid Allans £1.10.5. Went Grantham for chairs. Poured rain. Very dull. Martlew came.

Wed 30. Lovely day. Sunny and warm. Les has Silcock demonstration. Mary and Harold came Pegs.

Thu 31. Lovely day again for 2nd Silcock demonstration. Library. Mary and Harold came for sherry. WI coffee evening at Mrs Eli Coys. Bossie went shooting. Dull evening.

School Lane with the school building and Hall Farm to the left, before the War Memorial was erected. Mr Buxton is sitting on the motorbike, May Pick is standing. BTOW.

Green Lane about 1945, camping in Cyril Walker's Field, with Dan Coy's bell tent. From left to right standing - Pauline White (holding two boiled eggs), Glenys Coy (with the milk pail), Joyce Brown (holding an unidentified object), Shirley Stroud (with an unknown object), Margaret Hodges (with the kettle), sitting - Anne Lightfoot (with a plate of what may be nuts) and Mary Hodges (possibly peeling the potatoes). TCOY.

Harby: Village life in the Vale of Belvoir

August

Fri 1. Very dull morning. Close. End of day brighter. Michael came back. Robert started him in dairy. Went for drive to Long Bennington. Peg and Les went to Plungar Ba-B-Que.

Sat 2. Very close. Humid. Frank put up yard clock. Sue 21st birthday cowboy dance. Peg went with Mary and Harold.

Notes. Halfpenny out of circulation 1 August. Paid Allan £1 – 10 – 5d.

Daniel and Mary Coy with their daughter Ciss (Mary Alice) about 1902 doing the washing at the back of the house. Daniel is agitating the clothes in a tub with wooden tool called a dolly. Mary is rubbing the clothes to remove stubborn stains by hand. The 1901 census records Daniel employed in a cheese factory aged 40, the same age as his wife Mary, living in house 17 in the schedule with sons John Tom, Charles Edward, Alick and Daniel as well as his daughter. TCOY.

Exchange Row in Nether Street with the young Jim Towers on his toy horse and horse whip about 1928. The road surface is gravel rather than the macadam we know today. BTOW.

Harby: Village life in the Vale of Belvoir

Harby life

Charles Rawlinson on his tricycle with Peggy and, nearest the camera, Joan Rawlinson. At the entrance to Harby Lodge about 1930. JWAT.

In the garden of 42 Stathern Lane about 1940. From left to right, sitting Alice Hodges, Adela Reeves, Joseph Cunnington senior, with Marion Reeves standing at the front. NCUN.

At the back of 34 Stathern Lane in 1948, Mary Hodges on the left and Sheila Hodges. NCUN.

Harby: Village life in the Vale of Belvoir

SOME QUIET THOUGHTS
Tom Sadler, from Harby News issue 4 page 17.

The leaves flutter down, and the trees are gaunt and bare,
their naked branches reaching towards the sky, as if to declare
in defiance of the elements,
"We are ready for winter, your worst will not destroy us."

Soon the cold wind whistles in the lane, causing the leaves
to scurry along the ground,
together, in little groups, as though they have found
comfort and shelter in their togetherness.

Now the sky is overcast and the clouds, dark and heavy, shed their loads,
and gently, silently, the snowflakes ghost their way to earth,
covering the leaves, the fields, the roads,
and we know that winter is upon us.

Shyly the sun peeps through the empty clouds, with just a hint
of warmth, a promise of things to come,
a half-melted snowman stands helpless and pathetic on the lawn,
a reminder of the children's winter fun,
and gone are the leafy copses of yesterday.

Slowly, the trees once gaunt and bare, arouse, their slumbers o-er,
and from their waking branches appear,
as if by magic, the little buds, the infant leaves,
and nature's miracles are performed once more.

The hedgerows smile with flowers, the household fires, die,
the sunshine, now brighter, warms the air, and I think how lucky am I
to live in the country,
and what a pity that folk who are condemned to life in the city,
can only now and then share my vast fortune.

Cherry blossom in the garden of Elder House in the 1950s. CBOO.

NOTES ON THE CONTRIBUTORS

Nicola Biggadike, born in Harby in 1960, she was brought up in the village where her parents were much involved in the Cubs and Scouts.

Nora Blaze was born in 1908 in Nottingham. She married Wilson Blaze in 1932 and they spent some years in Jerusalem where she became a writer for womens magazines. They came to live in Harby in 1963 and she was the school secretary for some years. She became an authority and writer on local history. She died in 1992.

John Blundy, has lived in Harby since his dad, Harry Blundy, took up the job of village policeman in 1934. He married a girl from the nearby village of Scalford, Jackie Webster, and was a lecturer in auto engineering at Melton College.

Dora Butcher, born Mabbott in Harby in 1908, she lived in the village all her life, died in 1998. She married Jack Butcher in 1936 whose father was gamekeeper to the earl of Carnarvon and later landlord of the Nag's Head. She was active in Women's Institute and the church where Jack was church warden and much involved in bell ringing.

Edith Buxton was born in The Cross House opposite the school in 1892. She came to serve as infants' teacher in the school in 1912 and continued in the job until her retirement. She did not marry and lived in The Cross House until moving to a smaller dwelling after retirement. She died in 1972. She was organist in the church, active in the Women's Institute and a gifted entertainer.

Eli Coy, born in 1903, died in 1983 came from a well established Harby family. He worked in the ironstone mining on the Harby hills and was interested in history including the archaeological discoveries made during mining.

Henry Coy, born in 1928 and lived in Harby all his life. His father Isaac Coy ran a family business initially as a carrier with horse and cart and coal deliveries. This later expanded to a bus service and production of building materials.

Trevor Coy, born in Harby in 1933 and followed his father Dan Coy in his business as builder, plumber and tinsmith. They did much work for Harby Farmers' Dairy and Colston Bassett Dairy.

Leslie Cram, editor of the book, was born in Vancouver in 1942. He studied Archaeology and Anthropology at Cambridge University before a career as a museum curator. He is a Fellow of the Society of Antiquaries. He retired to Harby in 2000 to the house were his parents had lived since 1969.

Neil Cunnington, born in 1939 in the house that was once the old Marquis of Granby pub on Stathern Road and was brought up in Harby. After leaving school he worked for A.V.Roe at Langar airfield until the firm closed in 1968.

Notes on the contributors

Anne Dames, came to Harby with her husband John in 1951. She has been a parish councillor for forty years, and borough councillor. She was mayor of Melton 1989-90 and created an alderman.

John Dewey, born in Hose in 1928, married to Mary born in Plungar. He worked at A V Roe, Langar airfield and then ran a mobile green grocers van in Harby from 1960s. He was church warden and much involved in the British Legion.

Mark Dorrington, has lived in Harby since 2003. He studied Mediaeval History at the University of St Andrews and Archives Administration at the University of Wales, Aberystwyth. He is currently County Archivist for Nottinghamshire.

Jim Fisher's family originated from Harby in 1685. Jim was born in Nottingham in 1933. He married Pauline Wright of Harby. Jim's Grandmother was agent/organiser for the vale lace workers.

Betty Holyland, born Cooper in Harby in 1924, died 2010. Betty worked in the land army during the Second World War and as a nurse in London. She married and returned to Harby.

Tom Sadler was born at Brockenhurst in the New Forest in 1924. He came with RAF to Langar in 1944 and met a Harby girl, Muriel Scarborough. They married and moved to Watford where Tom was a policeman. They returned to Harby in early 1960s. Tom worked at PERA in Melton Mowbray and became parish councillor and Special Constable.

Peggy Shipman, 1919 to 2006, born Rawlinson, attended Melton grammar school, worked as a clerk at Harby and Stathern Station until her marriage to Leslie Shipman. They farmed at Stathern Lodge then Sherbrooke Farm.

Rex Stapleford, was born at Rotherby, Leics in 1932. His mother Caroline Isobel (nee Furmidge) was born in Harby. After leaving school he served an aircraft apprenticeship at A.V. Roe at Langar airfield. He resided at Harby from 1945 until leaving to further his career as a Mechanical Engineer in the mid-1950s.

Wendy Starbuck was born in 1944 in Harby and brought up in the village. She had two sons, Tim and Duncan, by her first marriage to Roger Cronin before meeting her second husband Steve McRobb. Wendy worked for many years as a special needs lecturer and counsellor at Melton College. She died in 2007 leaving four grandchildren.

Joan Watson, born Rawlinson in Harby in 1922, sister to Peggy Shipman. She married Robert Watson from the family who managed the dairy in Watsons Lane named after them. Robert was appointed manager of the firm. He was a parish, district and county councillor.

Molly Whittaker, 1910 to 1967, mother of Don Whittaker in the Harby History Group. His father ran a small farm on Stathern Lane.

SOURCES FOR THE HISTORY OF HARBY

compiled by Leslie Cram.

PLACES

The Record Office for Leicestershire, Leicester and Rutland holds sources on our village history including:- the school archive, Parish church archive, maps, trade directories, Harby Journal, Harby News.

Leicestershire County Council Libraries, Local Studies Resources holds past copies of newspapers.

WEBSITES

www.ancestry.co.uk. National Archives for the census returns and details of ancestors.
www.harby.co.uk. The village website where over a thousand photographs of old Harby can be seen including all those in this book.
www.historicaldirectories.org. Old trade directories.
www.meltonmowbray.steamrailways.com. Details of the railways and ironstone mining.

BOOKS

Anderson, John. 1976, Leicestershire Canals, bygones in camera. Privately printed.
British Geological Survey, 2002. Melton Mowbray. England and Wales sheet 142, solid and drift geology. 1:50,000 series. Keyworth, British Geological survey.
Burton, William. 1622. The Description of Leicestershire: Containing Matters of Antiquitye, Historye, Armorye, and Genealogy.
Carney, J N, K Ambrose and A Brandon. 2002. Geology of the Melton Mowbray district. Keyworth: British Geological Survey.
Chaworth-Musters, Mrs. 1890. A Cavalier Stronghold, a Romance of the Vale of Belvoir. London: Simpkin, Marshall, Hamilton, Kent & Co, Nottingham: James Bell.
Cox, Barrie. 2002. The Place-names of Leicestershire, part two, Framland Hundred, Nottingham: English Place-name Society.
Crabbe, George. 1795. "The Natural History of the Vale of Belvoir" in John Nichols "History and Antiquities of the County of Leicestershire" part 1.
Cram Leslie, Martin Henig and Keith Ambrose. 2005. A stone "celtic" human head from Harby, Leicestershire, Transactions of the Leicestershire Archaeological and Historical Society, 79, 91- 97.
Dale, T F. 1899. A history of the Belvoir Hunt. Westminster: Archibald Constable and Co.
Doyle Michael R P. 2009. Their name liveth for evermore : the Great War Roll of Honour for Leicestershire and Rutland, volumes 1 - 5. Published by Michael Doyle.
Drake 1861. Gazetteer and Directory of the Counties of Leicester and Rutland.

Sheffield.

Evelyn, Mary. 1927. The Cheese of the Country. Health, a Journal of Popular and Industrial Medicine, volume 6, number 40.

Franks, D L. 1974. Great Northern and London and North Western Joint Railway. Leeds: Turntable Enterprises.

Freeman, Roger A. 1994. UK Airfields of the Ninth: Then and Now. London: After the Battle.

Gill, Josiah. 1909. The History of Wesleyan Methodism in Melton Mowbray and the Vicinity, 1769-1909. Melton Mowbray: John Wartnaby Warner.

Goodwin, Barry and Raymonde Glynne Owen. 1994. 207 squadron RAF Langar, 1942 - 1943. York: Quack Books.

Halfpenny, Bruce Barrymore. 1991, Action Stations Volume 2: Military Airfields of Lincolnshire and the East Midlands. Patrick Stephens Ltd.

Henshaw, Alfred. 2003. The Great Northern Railway in the East Midlands: Nottingham - Grantham, Bottesford - Newark, Melton Mowbray, the Leicester Line and Ironstone Branches, Railway Correspondence and Travel Society

Hewlett, H B. 1979. The Quarries – ironstone, limestone and sand. Reprinted of the 1935 original in The Stantonian, The Magazine of the Stanton Ironworks Company Limited. Market Overton Industrial Railway Association, Cottesmore, Rutland.

Hickman, Trevor. 1992. Around Melton Mowbray in old photographs, Stroud: Nonsuch Publishing. Pocket edition 2007.

Hickman, Trevor. 1994. The Vale of Belvoir. Britain in old photographs, Stroud: Alan Sutton. Second edition 2004.

Hickman, Trevor. 1995. The History of Stilton cheese. Stroud: Alan Sutton.

Honeybone, Michael. 1987. The Vale of Belvoir. Buckingham: Barraccuda Books.

Kelly, A Lindsay. 1928. Directory of the Counties of Leicestershire and Rutland. London: Kelly's Directories.

Kelly, A Lindsay. 1941. Directory of the Counties of Leicestershire and Rutland. London: Kelly's Directories.

Lawton, Pam and Marilyn Garner. 2000, Minutes in Time, the Story of Harby Women's Institute. Nottingham: Fine Print.

Marrows, Hugh. 2003. The romantic canal, alongside the Grantham. Grantham Canal Partnership.

Nichols, John. 1795. History and Antiquities of the County of Leicestershire. Harby is mentioned in part ii pages 209-213, and 422, part iii page 534.

Pevsner, Nikolaus. revised by Elizabeth Williamson, second edition 1984. The buildings of England, Leicestershire and Rutland, London: Penguin Books, page 174.

Stapleford, Rex. 2006. A history of Harby cricket club 1919 to 1964. Privately printed.

Tonks Eric. 1992. The Ironstone Quarries of the Midlands, history, operations and railways, Part IX : Leicestershire. Cheltenham: Runpast Publishing.

White, William. 1846. History, Gazetteer, and Directory of Leicestershire. Sheffield.

INDEX

INDEX OF ILLUSTRATIONS. *Prepared by Leslie Cram*

This is an index to the illustrations in the book. It is divided into illustrations of people and general illustrations.

ILLUSTRATIONS OF PEOPLE

Adams, Arthur 77
Alderman, 157, 158
Allen, H 27

Baguley, George 21
Bailey 124
Banner, Jim 148
Beard, George 98
Beet, Kathleen 125
Bilby, 124
Blackwell, 124
Blundy, Anne 53, Elsie 141, Harry 94, Sarah 53
Booth, Cherry 135
Bremner, June 47
Brown, Arthur 101, Derek 149, 163, 164, Iris 151, John 101, Joyce 164, 172, Julia 47, 122, 164, Lizzie 101, Madge 163, May 164, Mrs 133, 141, Olive 76, Rose 101, Roy 149, 164, William 101
Butcher, Dora 133, 140, 141, 164, Jack 135, 140, 145, Woody 48
Buxton, Edith 29, 124, 133, Hilda 133, Mr 172, Pat 133

Chambers, Ken 98, Mrs 133, Valerie 144
Clark, Bernard, 164
Clarke, Jack 155
Comb, R 70
Cook, Mr 154, Walter 110
Cooper, Betty 42, Dorothy 42
Cox, Bertie 148
Coy, Alec 113, Billy 110, Billy Dan 110, Daniel 66, 172, 173, Eli 110, Elizabeth 40, Glenys 172, Henry Stokes 40, Isaac William 41, Mary 173, Mary Alice 173, Trevor 78, 113, Wendy 125, 144, William 94
Cunnington, Ada 102, Albert 102, Alice 54, 102, Doris 54, Gladys 54, 102, Joe 98, 174, Mr 108, Neil 119, 125, 144, 148
Curtis, Mark 110

Dames, Christopher 125
Dawson, Howard 125, Ian 125
Derby, Josie 47

Dewey, Ben 164, Gillian 125, Jane 125, Janet 164, John 107,
Dickman, Connie 76, 77, Mr 57, Mrs 141, Phyllis 76, 77, Thomas 110
Dransfield, Rev Joseph Henry 135

Eatherington, David 125, Harry 157
Edwards, Alfred Warman 29, 123, 124, 127, 153

Fairbrother, Eileen 51, Freda 51, 124, Herbert, 51, Jack 110, Mrs 141, Ruth 51, Sheila 51
Foster, Brenda 125, Claude 113, Derek 125
Furmidge, 33, 124, Geoff (Peg) 148, 157, Hilda 146, 149, 164, Ken 99, Mrs 141, Noel 148, 154, Olive Mary 124, Samuel 124, 153, 154

Gilder, Margaret 133
Gregg, Samuel 98
Grinnel Mrs 120
Grove, Ron 125
Groves, Peter 125

Hall, Michael 125
Hallam, Ann 125, Hector 110 Mary 125, Miss 139
Harriman, Mrs 141
Harwood Archibald Octavius 97, Nellie (Bunnie) 133
Haynes, Betty 151, George 98
Haywood, Bernard 154, 164, Ethel 75
Herrick, Annie 134, Thomas 26, Valerie 47
Hewitt, Tony 125
Hilsden, Ann 125
Hillsdon, Ann 151
Hodges, Alice 54, 174, Margaret 172, Mary 133, 172, 174, Sheila 133, 174
Holden, Alfred Cuthbert 135, 140
Holdsworth, Glyn 125, June 125
Hourd, Arthur 145, Charlie 154, Claude 164, Denis 164, Dennis (Hourdy) 157, John 125, 164, Sam 98, Twins 125
Howitt, 124, Annie 124
Hoyes, Mac 70, 135, 154
Hubbard, Peter 155

180   Harby: Village life in the Vale of Belvoir

Index

Jackson, Tommy 157, 158

Kemp, Harry (Gent) 86, Mrs 66, 100, Mary Ann 134, Nancy 146, Norman 146, Pam 47, Sheila 125
King, Lady 135
Kirk, Winifred 77

Lamin, Dorothy 104, Edward 104, John 104, Mrs 133, 140, Ron 133, 164
Lane, Eric 47, 125, 133
Leon, Mrs 141, Valerie 47, 122
Lightfoot, Anne 133, 172, Mrs 149
Looms, Gladys 54

Mabbott, William Alfred 91
Mackley, Bob 110, John 125, Mr 135, Mrs 133, Marion 47, 122, Phyllis 124
Manchester, Ernest 157, Herbert (Tilly) 98, Sheila 125, Stodge 149, Victoria 75
Marsden, Albert 158
Martin, Alan 125, Ernest 61, 110, 135
Martin, Lady 107
Mawson, Arthur 110
Millington, Vic 99
Moulds, Alec 124, Cecil 99, Christine 47, 144, Colin 47, 155, Frank 164, Hilda 164, Jim 107, 110, 145, L 70, Linda 125, Mr 36, Mrs 133, 141, Ralph 164, Rose 164, Stan 158
Munro, Ted 99
Musson, Amy 42, B K 130, Charlie 155, Matilda 29, 123, 127, R (Cracker) 157, 158

Newton, Bill 154, Mrs 141, Pidge 146, 149, 164
Norman, James, 25, 166, Rev Manners Octavius 134, 166,

O'Brien, Pat 79
O'Leary, Michael 98, 99, 158
Osborne, Andrew 125
Oxbrough, Flo 133, 141, 163, Jess 145

Palmer, Bernard 125
Partridge, Patsy 125
Payne, George 135, John 146
Pearson, Dorothy 98, Mrs 125
Pepper, Betty 133, Bill 110, Christine 133, Frederick 102, Jack 102, 158, Lizzie 102
Pick, Enid 141, Len 110, May 172, Walter 110, 154
Pizer, Bunny 158
Potter, Marion 69
Powell-Hughes, Rev Ieuan Delvin 135

Prichett, "Dick" 120
Pritchett, Anthea 47, Reg 98, 135
Pym, Charley, 164, Joyce 164
Pymm, Stuart 125

Rawlings, Claude 154, Jim 110, 154, Madge 124, Mary 47, May 124, Pearl 151, Thelma 47, 144, Winston 125
Rawlinson, Charles 174, Joan, 74, Peggy, 174, Vera (Queen), 88
Reeves, Adela 174, Marion 174, Mr 51, Nigel 98
Richmond, Alf 157, 158, Michael 157
Rimmington, Len 98
Robinson, Frank 157

Savige, Rev John Sydney 135
Scarborough, Harry 158, Nell 141
Seal, Jennifer 125
Sharp, Bill 135
Shipman, Harry 158, Leslie 85, 146, 158, Peggy 146, Tony 125
Slater, Ian 47, 155, Iris 148, Colin 125, 144, Linda 125, Margaret 47, Ron 125
Smith, Jack (Trigger) 157
Staniforth, Chris 75
Stapleford, Anne 133, Belle 120, Carole 133, Jean 133, Peter 155, Rex 113
Starbuck, Betty 38, 77, Harry 102, Henry 19, Mary Jane 38, 73, Samuel, 110, Wendy 47
Stead, Barbara 138, Mabel, 103, Martin Sunderland 59, 62
Stokes, John 77, Thomas 110, Winifred 124
Stone, Rev Edward Henry 134
Stroud, Shirley 172

Thomlinson, Richard 125
Thomson, Adela 133
Thorpe, Cheryl 125
Tinsley, Anne 125, 133, Carol 47, Dick 164, Mary 125, Pam 125, Robert 125
Tomlinson, C 61, Celia 122, Mrs 133
Towers, Ernie 91, 110, 154, Jim 149, 155, 163, 173, Jimmy 164, Matt 102, Matthew 93, May 38, 146, 163, 164, 170, Sam 47, 122, 133, 155
Townsend, Susan 53

Vernon Smith, Guy 133

Walker, Ben 155, Cherry 151, Cyril 172, John 155, Mrs 133
Ward 124, Derek 155, 164, Dorothy 124

Harby: Village life in the Vale of Belvoir

Index

Waring, Jennifer 47, Ruby 133
Wass, Mrs 164, Steve 164
Watchorn, Cis 45, Lil 36
Watson, Mr 110, Mrs Mabel Alice, 139, 141, Robert 75
White, Diane 47, Ellis 124, 148, 158, 160, Nance 124, Pauline 172
Whitehead 103
Whittaker, Don 83, 149, 150, 164, Leslie (Pudding) 83, 110, 148, Molly, 80, 148
Whittle 124, Michael 125, Olive 124, Wendy 53, 125
Widdowson, Sam 99
Wiles, Tom 110
Wilcox, Stan 148
Wilford 124, Brian (Farmer) 157, 158, Cliff 124, John (Bufton) 157, 158
Wilkinson, Mrs Walter 120
Williams, Mr 110
Wills, Mr 77
Wilson, Noel 135, Tommy 47
Wood, Guilford 32, 34, 105, 127
Wright, Avis 133, 141, 146, James 138, Jane 125, Janet 146, Mrs 36, 141, Pauline 47, Sylvia 141, 151
Wyles 103

GENERAL INDEX

Allotments 53,
A V Roe 120, 149

Barnstone 99, 118
Bellringers 135
Belvoir Hunt 161
Blacksmith 27, 59, 62, 103
Box Bush 66, 78
Boy scouts 150
Boyers Orchard, 26, 51, 53
Bradwell's shop 103
Browns shop, 101
Burden Lane 36, 102, 125
Butcher 27

Canal , 25, 31, 69, 70, 162
Canteen ladies 120
Cart 27, 33, 36, 61, 101
Cheese making, 3, 75, 76, 77, 78, 84
Christmas Fayre 133, 135
Church 13, 55, 127, 128, 129, 130, 133, 135, 161
Church plan 130
Church warden 93
Clipping the church 53

Colston Lane, 55, 158, 160
Colston Bridge 104
Combine harvester 85
Cricket 153- 156

Dairy, see cheese making
Dickmans Cottage 51, 57
Dickmans Lane 57

Elder House 175
Exchange Row 173
Excursions 141, 163, 164

Farmhouse 32, 79, 156, 160
Farming 33, 82, 83 - 86, 88
Flower Service 53, 133
Font 13
Football 157, 158, 160
Forge 27, 59, 62
Fox hunting, 161

Garden Fete/Party 134, 140
Girl guides 151
Great Yarmouth 141
Green Lane 54, 102, 172

Hall Farm 33, 156, 166
Harby and Stathern Station 97, 98
Harby and Stathern United 158
Harby Famers' Dairy 78
Harby Lodge Farm 79, 86, 88, 174
Harby Observer Corps 110
Harriman's Store 55
Harvest Festival 138
Heavy horses 86
Horticultural Show 166

Incline 90, 91
Ironstone, 91

Langar airfield, 118 – 120, 149
Langar Bridge, 25, 31, 162

Mackley's Orchard 53
Main Street 38, 52, 55, 148
Map, 1790 11, 1793 12, 1884 23, 1904 30, 1906 8, 1930 39, 1950s 82, 1952 49, 1971 58
Marquis of Granby 147
Methodist Chapel, 136, 137, 138, 148
Milk 36, 52, 84, 85, 104

Nag's Head 149
Nether Street 25, 27, 40, 55, 102, 173

Pantomime 144
Pinfold Lane, 36
Poplars paddock 52
Post Office 36, 100, 102

Railway, 90, 91, 97- 99
Rectory 13, 26, 34, 134, 140, 162
Rogation parade 133
Rutland Terrace 54

School 27, 29, 47, 48, 51, 108, 115, 121 - 127, 133, 144, 172
School Lane 21, 27, 28, 32, 36, 48, 51, 59, 62, 94, 123 – 125, 172
Sherbrooke Farm 55, 85, 160
Shops 55, 100 – 103
Skating 25, 31, 162
Skegness 163
Slaughter house 102
Smithy, see forge
Starbuck House 19, 38
Stathern Lane/Road 24, 27, 28, 52, 83, 99, 102, 147, 174
Steppings Lane 66
Sunday school 133
Swimming 70

Tennis 134, 162
Thraves Terrace 38
Tin school 121

Village Hall/Men's Institute/Reading Room 113, 133, 135, 139, 141, 144, 145, 146

War Memorial 13, 103, 105, 108
Watsons Lane 26, 32, 45, 94, 100
Wharflands 170
Wheelwright 61
White Hart, 92, 148
Whitewoods 27, 28
Whittaker's Farm 80, 83, 84
Windmill 104
Women's Institute 139, 140, 141
Women's Volunteer Service 115
Wong 51, 69, 70